ARE SKETCHES™

VOLUME I

A Visual Study Guide to the Architect Registration Exams

Lora Nicole Teagarden, AIA, LEED AP BD+C®

*To my family who taught a young girl to
go after her dreams.*

CONTENTS

Introduction
How to use this book and get licensed.

Sketches
The sketches cover PPP: the Programming, Planning, & Practice portion of testing. You may see overlap into CDS - Contract Documents & Services, SPD - Site Planning & Design, and other sections of the test. Similarly, there is information within those sections that you will see on this test as well.

Each sketch can be studied quickly, the intent being that each sketch creates a bite-sized piece of information on the testing material. Each sketch also has a short, defining blurb of information below.

Study hard. You can do this.

HOW TO USE THIS BOOK AND GET LICENSED

"Insert wise sayings here"

...that's literally what I put as a placeholder while finishing the sketches for this first book. The truth is that getting your license is one of the biggest undertakings you will experience in your life, but it doesn't have to be exceptionally hard or scary. Each person's path to licensure will be different, but the goal of this book is to help make the process a little easier.

In talking with a friend about the process of studying after I completed my tests, I told him that I would read through the study material but find myself sketching out the idea to make sure I understood the verbiage. He said he tended towards the same thing on occasion. I talked to others who expressed interest in seeing the sketches...and AREsketches™ was born.

Architects are visual people, but so much of the study material is word-based. With ongiong changes to the ARE format, this visual aspect will be even more important to understand. As I thought more about this afterwards, I decided to take my sketches and refine them for sharing. I have been slowly sharing them on Instagram with the hashtag #AREsketches and hosting them on my website. After gathering a bit of a following from those taking their tests or simply interested in architecture, I decided to gather and focus all the information in a book to help those interested in a physical form of the sketches.

Consider it a flipbook. A sketchbook. A study guide. It, as well as your path to licensure, is entirely up to you and what you make of it. Each sketch should take 30 seconds to a couple minutes to understand, some being more complex than others. Read one, or 5, a day. Read 10. Read it all in a day. Scribble in the margins, create your own sketches alongside the ones in this book...mark it up as you please. Dog-ear the pages or don't. Maybe go crazy with post-its or tab devices. The world is your oyster.

Seriously, I know all that sounds funny, but you know best how you retain and comprehend material. So do what you need to with this book because the point is licensure... the shiny pot of gold at the end of the long rainbow that is testing. It does exist, and you will be an architect. I believe in you and hopefully this book will help.

I get a handful of emails each week from people just like you, working hard towards getting their license. I love hearing from them and I love being able to help. That is the root of where this book was born - because a young licensed architect empowered to make the world better is net positive, so if you ever have any questions or just want to drop me a line - please don't hesitate. To that end, I've listed below all of the places you can find me. The goal is to get you licensed and I'm excited to be on this journey with you. Good luck!

Lora

Website: www.L-2-Design.com
Twitter: @L2DesignLLC
Instagram: @L2DesignLLC
Facebook: https://www.facebook.com/L.2.design.llc/

BIG TO SMALL:
LARGER ENVIRONMENT
AFFECTS SITE & BUILDING
DESIGN

CONTEXT

SMALL TO BIG:
FINISHED BUILDING &
SITE AFFECTS COMMUNITY

How do buildings play a part in their surroundings? Context. It's a concept that goes both ways.

1

FIRST SETTLEMENTS:

AMOEBIC, HAPHAZARD LAYOUT. IMPORTANT PIECES @ CENTER OF VILLAGE.

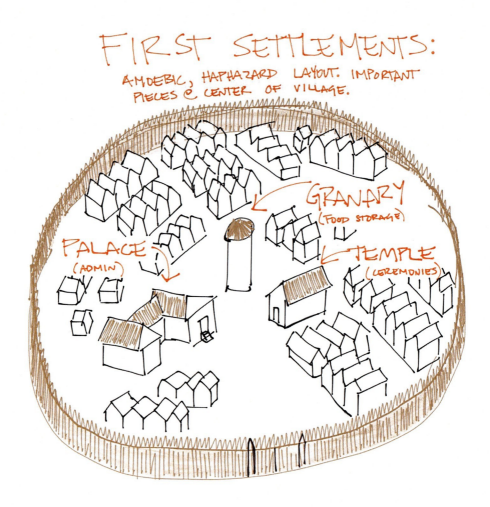

GRANARY (FOOD STORAGE)

PALACE (ADMIN)

TEMPLE (CEREMONIES)

The first settlements were haphazardly laid out with food, religion, and administration at the center.

GREEK CITIES

MORE HIGHLY DEVELOPED.

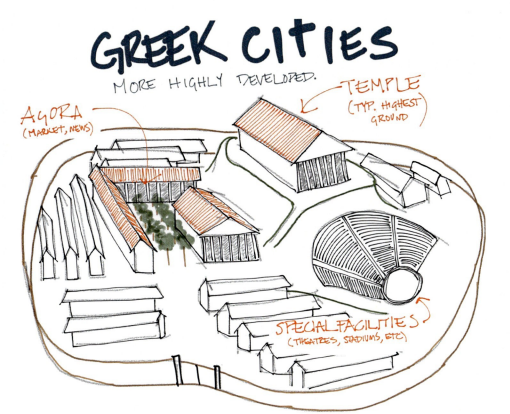

AGORA
(MARKET, NEWS)

TEMPLE
(TYP. HIGHEST
GROUND)

SPECIAL FACILITIES
(THEATRES, STADIUMS, ETC)

Greek cities began to think longer term in development. They focused not only on faith but also on market and facilities to help improve community.

MEDIEVAL CITIES
MAIN CROSSROADS + INFORMAL / IRREGULAR STREETS

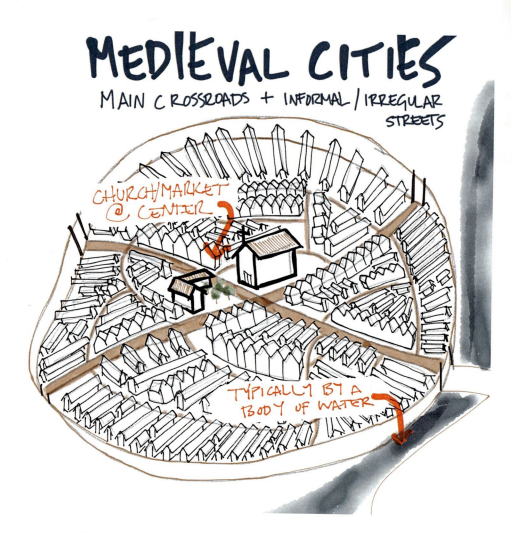

CHURCH/MARKET @ CENTER

TYPICALLY BY A BODY OF WATER

Medieval cities began to see more crossroads and informal structures due to movement of carts and beginning thoughts towards repetition.

MEDIEVAL PT. 2

GUNPOWDER CHANGES EVERYTHING.

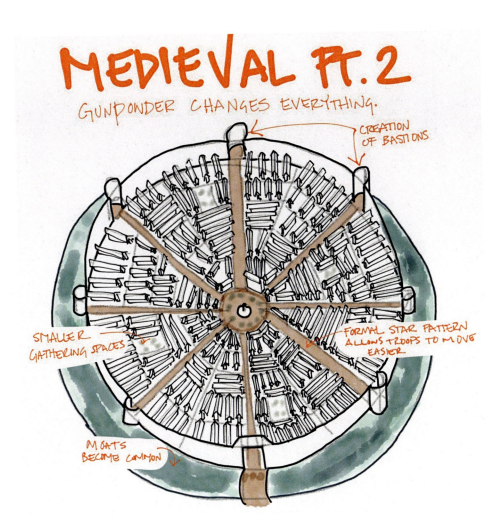

CREATION OF BASTIONS

SMALLER GATHERING SPACES

FORMAL STAR PATTERN ALLOWS TROOPS TO MOVE EASIER

MOATS BECOME COMMON

Then comes gunpowder. Cities began to focus on protecting those within their walls, creating formal star patterns for quick access to turrets or safety.

Renaissance Period

- DEFENSE IMPORTANT, BUT **AESTHETIC** PRIORITY
- RADIAL BOULEVARDS + SECONDARY STREETS
- VISTAS!

LONDON

IMPORTANT NODES

THAMES

SIR CHRISTOPHER
WREN

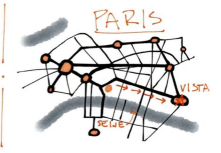

PARIS

VISTA

SEINE

GEORGES - EUGENE
HAUSSMANN

The Renaissance Period of planning started bringing in thoughts of aesthetic with tree and building-lined boulevards to point towards vistas, framing spaces.

CAMILLO SITTE

AUSTRIAN ARCHITECT / TOWN PLANNER

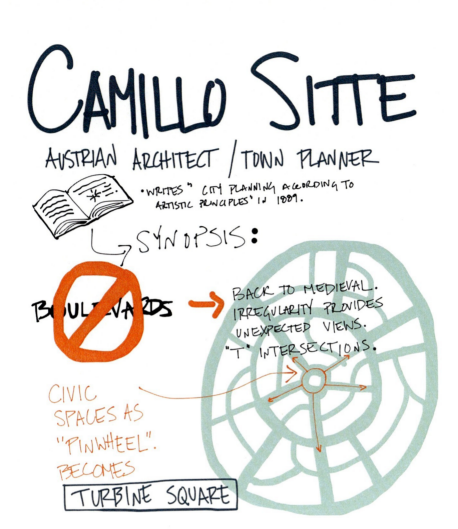

• WRITES "CITY PLANNING ACCORDING TO ARTISTIC PRINCIPLES" IN 1889.

↳ SYNOPSIS:

BOULEVARDS → BACK TO MEDIEVAL. IRREGULARITY PROVIDES UNEXPECTED VIEWS. "T" INTERSECTIONS.

CIVIC SPACES AS "PINWHEEL". BECOMES
TURBINE SQUARE

Camillo Sitte, an Austrian architect, decides city planning should be more informal and irregular than that of his renaissance brothers.

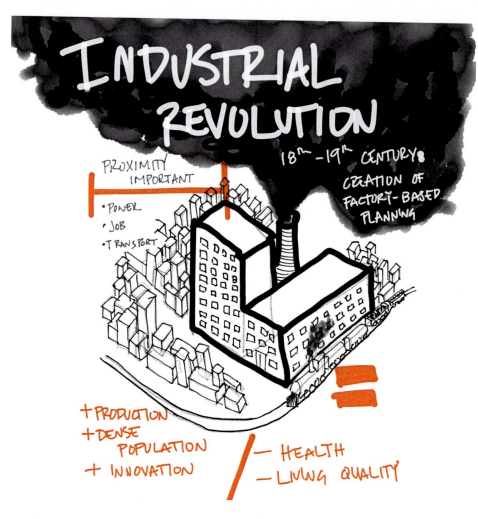

The industrial revolution brought not only progress, but also harm in city planning.

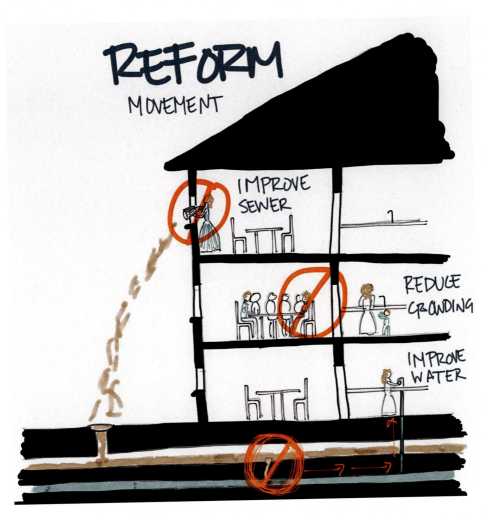

The reform movement aimed to fix issues that arose during the industrial revolution.

GARDEN CITY

EBENEZER HOWARD - 1898

BEST OF CITY + COUNTRY IN 6,000 ACRES

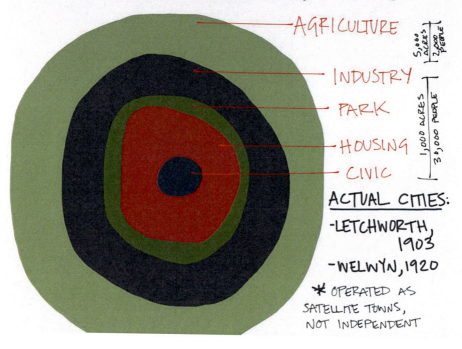

AGRICULTURE

INDUSTRY

PARK

HOUSING

CIVIC

5,000 ACRES | 2,000 PEOPLE

1,000 ACRES | 30,000 PEOPLE

<u>ACTUAL CITIES:</u>

-LETCHWORTH, 1903

-WELWYN, 1920

✳ OPERATED AS SATELLITE TOWNS, NOT INDEPENDENT

After the Industrial Revolution, designers attempted to plan cities to include urban + agriculture; hoped to be self-sustaining.

CITÉ INDUSTRIELLE

— TONY GARNIER, 1917, FRANCE

— 35,000 PEOPLE

＊ FIRST MAJOR STEPS TOWARDS ZONING.

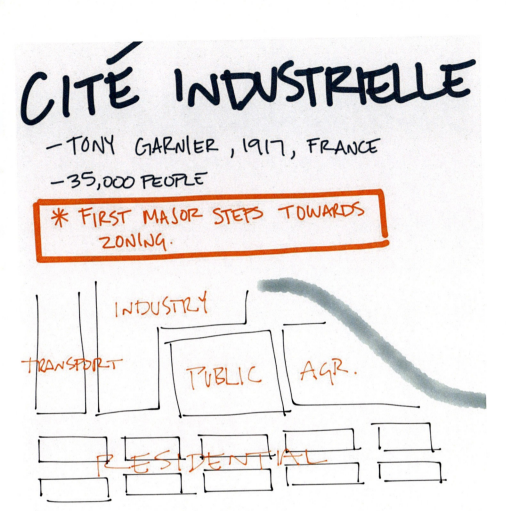

The Cite Industrielle, though unbuilt, took the first major steps towards zoning.

U.S.A. PLANNING

-MELTING POT ALSO IMPACTS PLANNING;
  DIVERSE PEOPLE = DIVERSE IDEAS/STYLES
- AGRARIAN LIFESTYLE

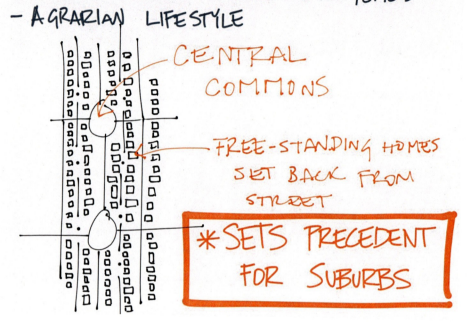

CENTRAL COMMONS

FREE-STANDING HOMES
SET BACK FROM
STREET

*SETS PRECEDENT
FOR SUBURBS

As people from different countries moved to the US, they brought their planning ideas with them.

THE GRIDIRON

- PHILADELPHIA, 1682
- REGULARLY PLANNED OPEN SPACES, UNIFORM SPACING & SETBACKS

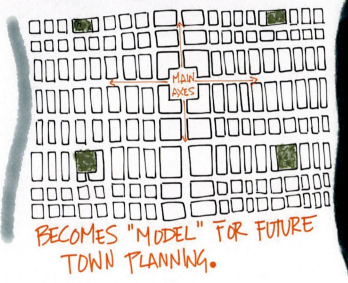

MAIN AXES

BECOMES "MODEL" FOR FUTURE TOWN PLANNING.

The Gridiron in Philadelphia creates a model for future town planing.

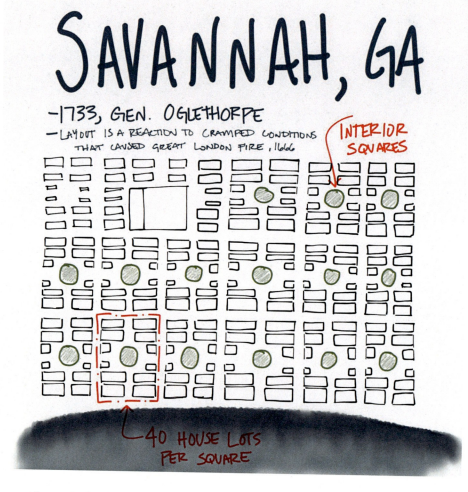

SAVANNAH, GA

- 1733, GEN. OGLETHORPE
- LAYOUT IS A REACTION TO CRAMPED CONDITIONS THAT CAUSED GREAT LONDON FIRE, 1666

INTERIOR SQUARES

40 HOUSE LOTS PER SQUARE

The Oglethorpe plan was in response to the Great London Fire.

ORDINANCE
— OF 1785 —

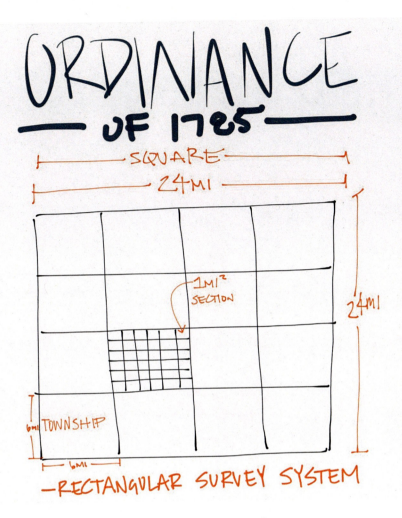

SQUARE
24 MI

1 MI² SECTION

24 MI

TOWNSHIP
6 MI
6 MI

—RECTANGULAR SURVEY SYSTEM

The Ordinance of 1785 established a universal zoning parameter via a grid system.

AMERICA'S Capitol

PIERRE L'ENFANT

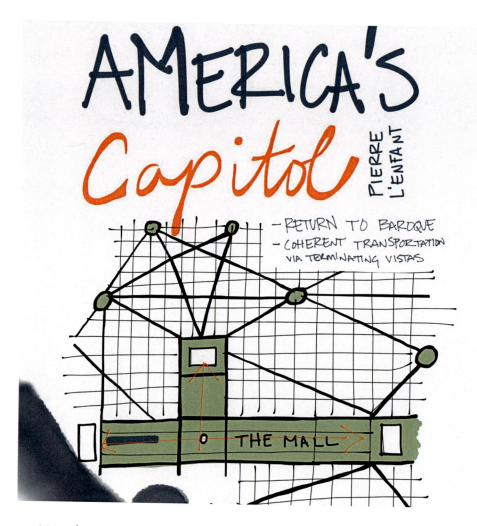

- RETURN TO BAROQUE
- COHERENT TRANSPORTATION VIA TERMINATING VISTAS

THE MALL

Washington D.C.'s master plan by L'Enfant returned to Baroque planning with boulevards and vistas.

Olmstead

-FREDERICK LAW OLMSTEAD - ONE OF FIRST
LANDSCAPE ARCHITECTS TO PRESERVE &
IMPLEMENT NATURAL FEATURES

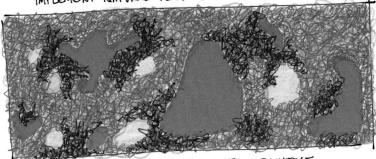

-CENTRAL PARK COMPLETED WITH ARCHITECT
CALVERT VAUX -1850's

OTHER PARKS BY OLMSTEAD

-PROSPECT PARK,
   BROOKLYN

- RIVERSIDE PARK,
   NEW YORK

- AUDOBON PARK,
   NOLA

- MET. PARK SYSTEMS,
   BOSTON

Olmstead was one of the first to gain recognition for preserving natural features and subsequently planned a number of parks and towns throughout the United States.

Columbian
EXPOSITION

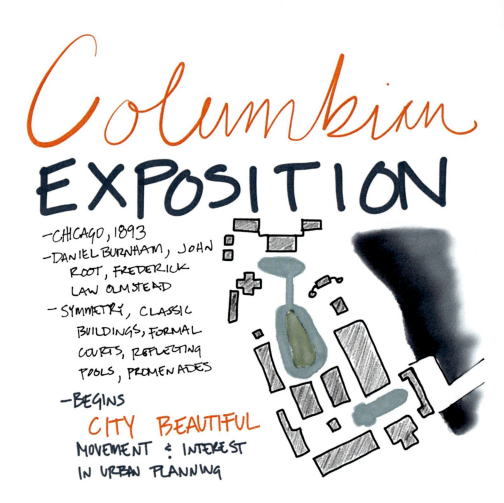

- CHICAGO, 1893
- DANIEL BURNHAM, JOHN
    ROOT, FREDERICK
    LAW OLMSTEAD
- SYMMETRY, CLASSIC
    BUILDINGS, FORMAL
    COURTS, REFLECTING
    POOLS, PROMENADES

- BEGINS
    CITY BEAUTIFUL
MOVEMENT & INTEREST
IN URBAN PLANNING

The Columbian Exposition at the 1893 World's Fair in Chicago started the City Beautiful movement.

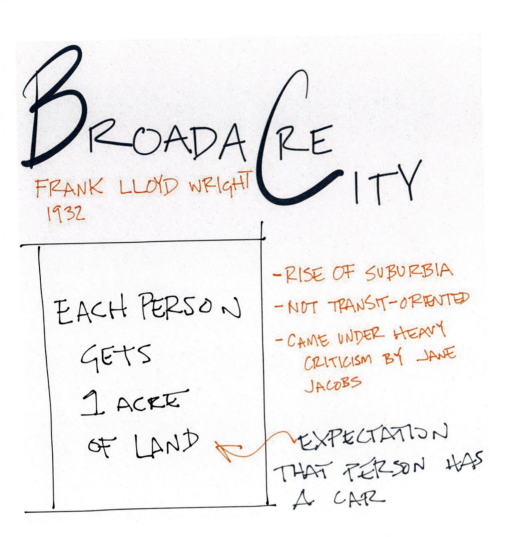

BROADACRE CITY

FRANK LLOYD WRIGHT
1932

EACH PERSON
GETS
1 ACRE
OF LAND

- RISE OF SUBURBIA
- NOT TRANSIT-ORIENTED
- CAME UNDER HEAVY
  CRITICISM BY JANE
  JACOBS

EXPECTATION
THAT PERSON HAS
A CAR

We all love Frank, but Broadacre City sadly
forecasted suburbia…

Corbu tried his hand at urban planning in the 1930's with the Radiant City concept.

NEW

HOUSING
SHOPPING
BUSINESS

- 1940s
- AUTONOMOUS

- POPULATION
INCREASED
30K→70→
250K
← GREENBELT

TOWN

In the 1940's in England, they came up with an autonomous "New Town" concept.

The New Town concept was brought to the US as well, but neither continent could make it autonomous. Lucky for us, living in a bubble didn't work well.

NEW URBANISM

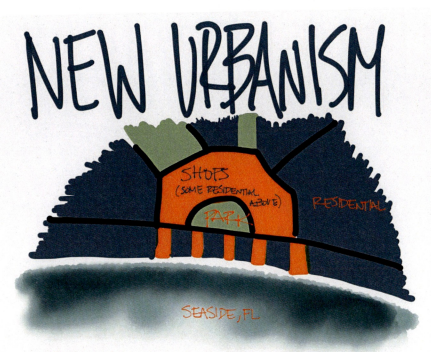

SHOPS
(SOME RESIDENTIAL
ABOVE)

RESIDENTIAL

PARK

SEASIDE, FL

- BUILDING, NEIGHBORHOOD, DISTRICT, ⅋ REGIONAL INTERACTION
- MIXED USE: VARIETY OF HOUSING TYPES WITHIN WALKING DISTANCE OF SHOPS ⅋ OFFICES

 The recent planning style of New Urbanism looks at providing everything one needs on a neighborhood scale.

DEVELOPMENT

GENERALLY DETERMINED BY GEOGRAPHICAL FEATURES & LAYOUT OF TRANSPORTATION.

Patterns

The development patterns of a city or town can be created around geography, transportation, or standard grid patterns.

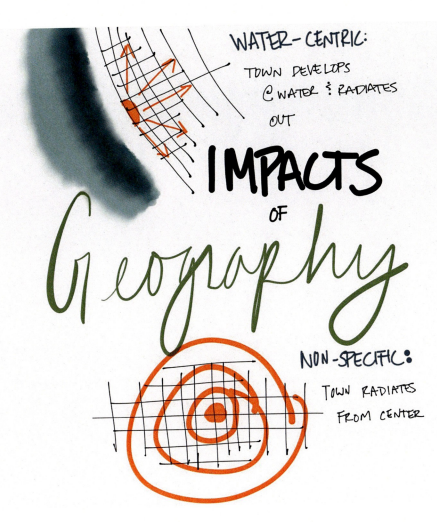

WATER-CENTRIC:
TOWN DEVELOPS
℮ WATER & RADIATES
OUT

IMPACTS
OF
Geography

NON-SPECIFIC:
TOWN RADIATES
FROM CENTER

This may seem like a no-brainer, but geography impacts city planning more than you think.

EXPANDING Grid

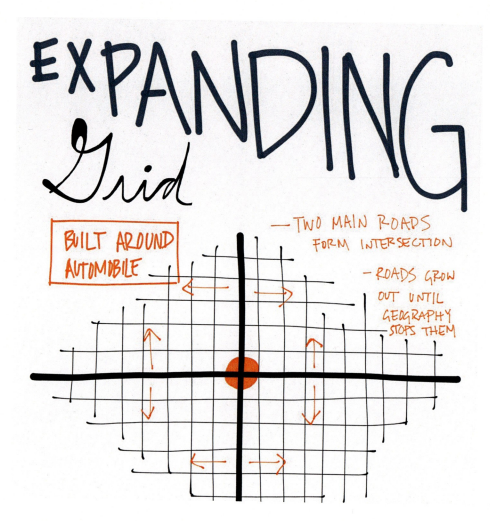

BUILT AROUND AUTOMOBILE

— TWO MAIN ROADS FORM INTERSECTION

— ROADS GROW OUT UNTIL GEOGRAPHY STOPS THEM

The pattern of the expanding grid radiates out from a central point in n-s/e-w streets.

Star Pattern

RADIATING SPOKES
OF MASS TRANSIT
HIGHWAYS

URBAN
CORE

LOWER DENSITY
DEVELOPMENT

The star pattern has radiating arms like bicycle spokes.

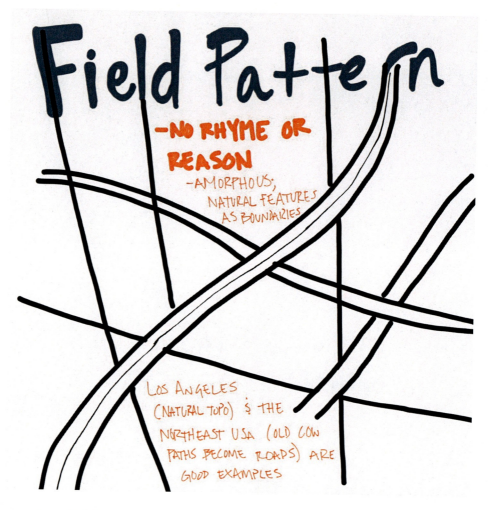

Field Pattern

—NO RHYME OR REASON

—AMORPHOUS; NATURAL FEATURES AS BOUNDARIES

LOS ANGELES (NATURAL TOPO) & THE NORTHEAST USA (OLD COW PATHS BECOME ROADS) ARE GOOD EXAMPLES

The field pattern traces old cow and farm paths. You can find it frequently in old European and New England towns.

SATELLITE

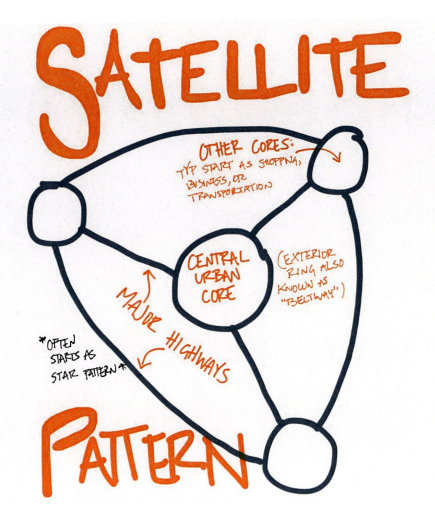

OTHER CORES:
TYP START AS SHOPPING, BUSINESS, OR TRANSPORTATION

CENTRAL URBAN CORE

(EXTERIOR RING ALSO KNOWN AS "BELTWAY")

MAJOR HIGHWAYS

OFTEN STARTS AS STAR PATTERN

PATTERN

The satellite pattern connects a major urban core to smaller suburban cores via highway.

Megalopolis

2+ MAJOR URBAN CENTERS:

GROW TOGETHER AS THE SPACE BETWEEN IS DEVELOPED.

SECTIONS OF NORTHEAST USA AND SOUTHERN CALIFORNIA TAKE ON THIS PATTERN.

A Megalopolis happens when multiple large cities grow together.

Imageability

KEVIN LYNCH

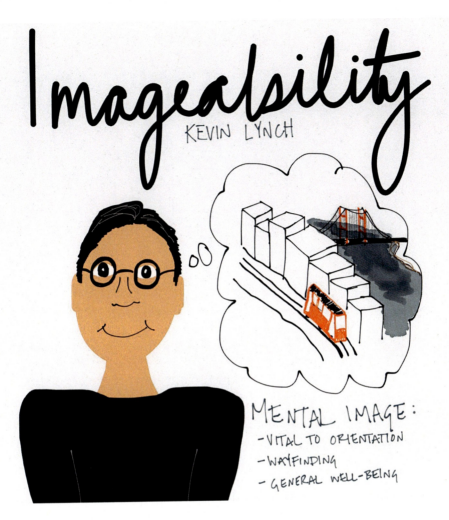

MENTAL IMAGE:
- VITAL TO ORIENTATION
- WAYFINDING
- GENERAL WELL-BEING

Imageability is the mental image each person creates of a city that helps with wayfinding or their overall perception of the environment.

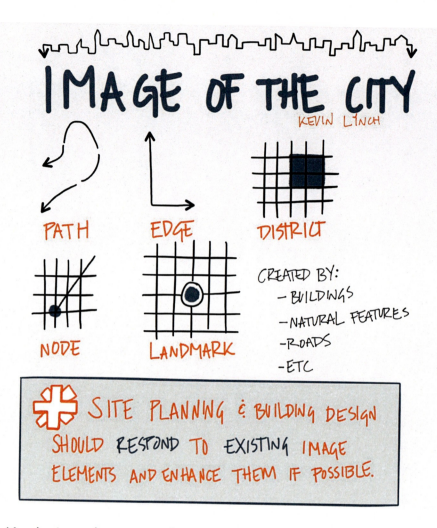

IMAGE OF THE CITY

KEVIN LYNCH

PATH   EDGE   DISTRICT

NODE   LANDMARK

CREATED BY:
- BUILDINGS
- NATURAL FEATURES
- ROADS
- ETC

SITE PLANNING & BUILDING DESIGN SHOULD RESPOND TO EXISTING IMAGE ELEMENTS AND ENHANCE THEM IF POSSIBLE.

Kevin Lynch wrote the "Image of the city", explaining the different planning elements and how they impact a person's view and use of a city.

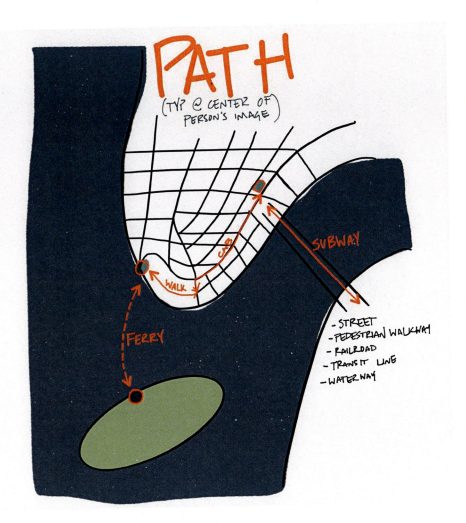

The first of the planning elements that shape your view of the city is the path.

EDGE

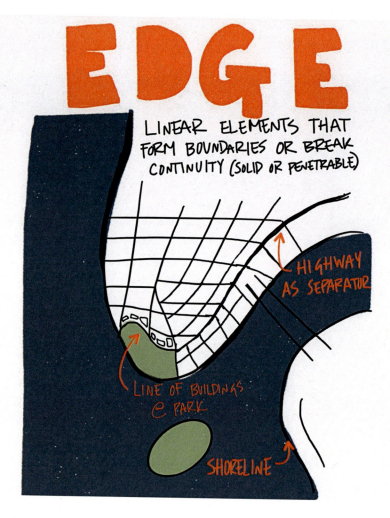

LINEAR ELEMENTS THAT FORM BOUNDARIES OR BREAK CONTINUITY (SOLID OR PENETRABLE)

HIGHWAY AS SEPARATOR

LINE OF BUILDINGS @ PARK

SHORELINE

There are a variety of things that can act like an edge. Can you think of more? Draw them below!

District

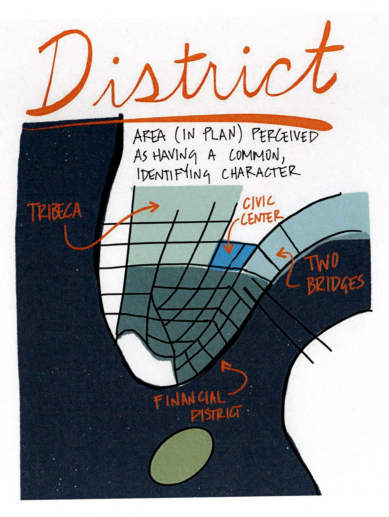

AREA (IN PLAN) PERCEIVED AS HAVING A COMMON, IDENTIFYING CHARACTER

TRIBECA

CIVIC CENTER

TWO BRIDGES

FINANCIAL DISTRICT

NYC is known for its districts, but did you ever really know what that meant.

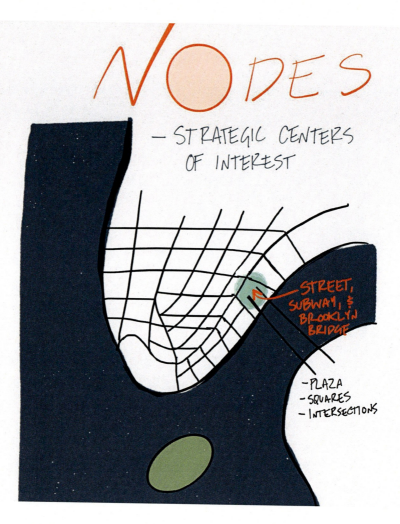

NODES

— STRATEGIC CENTERS OF INTEREST

STREET, SUBWAY, & BROOKLYN BRIDGE

—PLAZA
—SQUARES
—INTERSECTIONS

A node becomes labeled as such when it becomes a point of interest (that can be entered).

Landmark

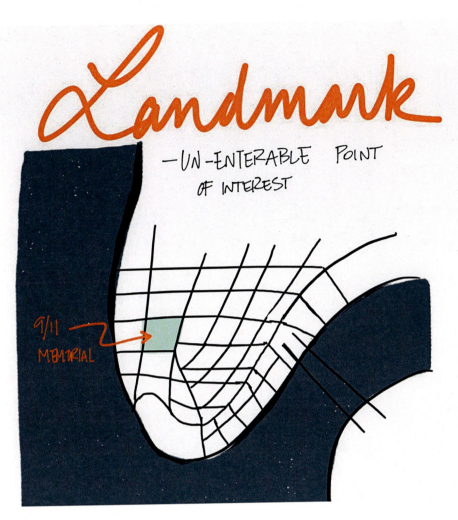

—UN-ENTERABLE POINT OF INTEREST

9/11 MEMORIAL

Landmarks help with wayfinding. They are a point of interest that draws people to a place, but one you cannot enter. (Think the waterfalls of the 9/11 memorial)

Other Neighborhood

- TYPICALLY FOLLOWS STREET PATTERNS
- BLOCKS SUBDIVIDED TO LOT
- LOTS HAVE OWN IDENTITY

FOUNTAINS

TOWN HALL

SMALL ESPLANADES

Planning Strategies

There are other design pieces that go into neighborhood planning to increase livability.

SUPERBLOCK

- FROM NEW TOWN CONCEPTS
- FIRST TEST: RADBURN, NJ -
  HENRY WRIGHT
- LIMIT CARS, INCREASE PEDESTRIAN

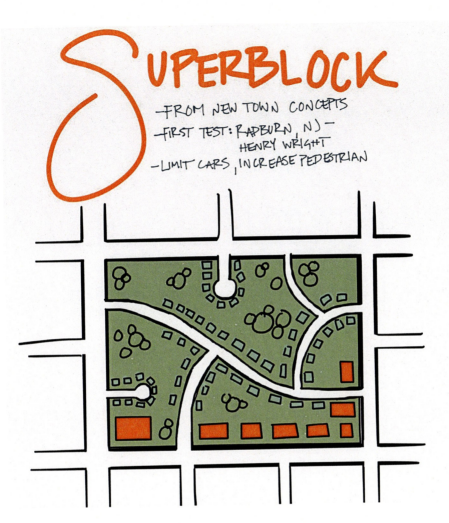

The Superblock formed from the new town concepts. Many larger planning communities, like multi-stage retirement facilities, operate on this idea.

SUPERBLOCK PROBLEMS

— CORBU & NIEMEYER ATTEMPTED VERSIONS
— LIFE REVOLVES AROUND AUTOMOBILE
— DRIVES CAUSE SEPARATION NOT INCLUSION

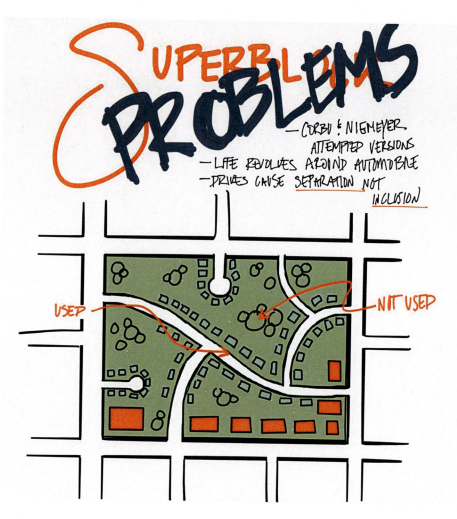

USED — NOT USED

The Superblock is not without its problems, though. If you want or need to go elsewhere, your life revolves around the automobile. This need then puts the car, not the human, front and center.

PLANNED UNIT DEVELOPMENT

— EACH PARCEL HAS MIX OF USES:
  RESIDENTIAL, COMMERCIAL,
  RECREATIONAL, ETC
— VARIABLE DENSITIES

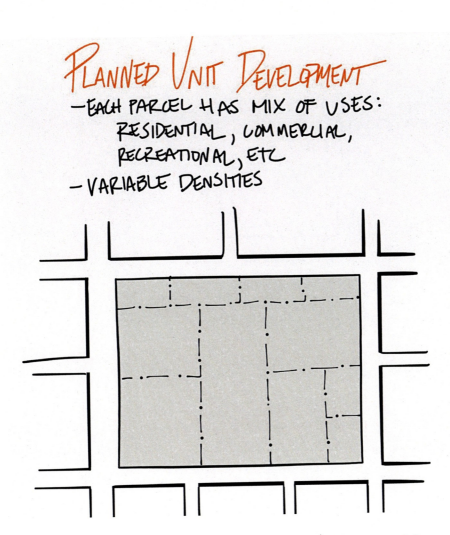

The planned unit development tried to provide density and a mix of uses to the superblock.

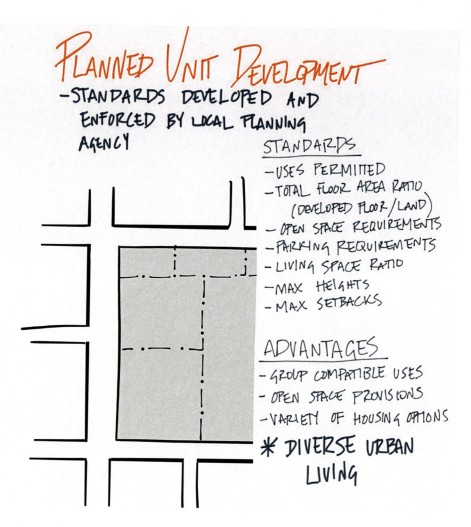

PLANNED UNIT DEVELOPMENT
- STANDARDS DEVELOPED AND ENFORCED BY LOCAL PLANNING AGENCY

STANDARDS
- USES PERMITTED
- TOTAL FLOOR AREA RATIO (DEVELOPED FLOOR / LAND)
- OPEN SPACE REQUIREMENTS
- PARKING REQUIREMENTS
- LIVING SPACE RATIO
- MAX HEIGHTS
- MAX SETBACKS

ADVANTAGES
- GROUP COMPATIBLE USES
- OPEN SPACE PROVISIONS
- VARIETY OF HOUSING OPTIONS

* DIVERSE URBAN LIVING

The Planned Unit Development has some advantages - standards being one of them.

DEVELOPMENT PATTERN:
DENSITY

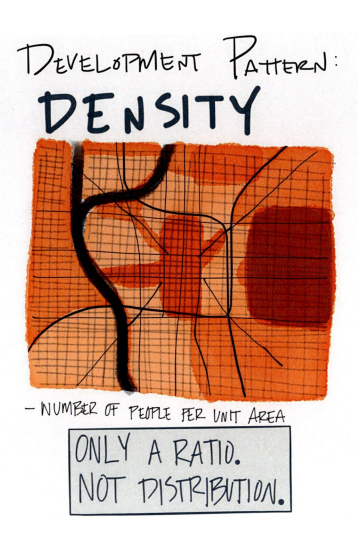

— NUMBER OF PEOPLE PER UNIT AREA

ONLY A RATIO.
NOT DISTRIBUTION.

Density is a ratio - it doesn't tell if the person is right next to 5 others or if they're equally spaced within 500sf.

DENSITY ≠ CROWDS

DENSITY DOESN'T SHOW DISTRIBUTION = HOW PEOPLE LIVE WITHIN THE AREA.

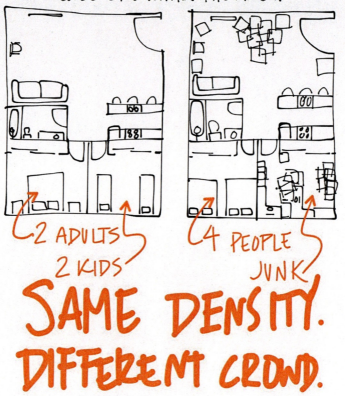

2 ADULTS
2 KIDS

4 PEOPLE
JUNK

SAME DENSITY.
DIFFERENT CROWD.

I repeat: density doesn't show how people are distributed through a space. It's important to remember that it's just a ratio.

CULTURE HELPS DETERMINE DENSITY COMFORT

NOLA: 2,029 PPL/SQ.MI
HOT & HUMID. CHEAP LAND.
MINIMAL MID-RISE.

NYC: 27,012 PPL/SQ.MI
LIMITED SPACE. LOTS OF
HIGH-RISE. LAND IS $$$.

SEATTLE: 7,251 PPL/SQ.MI
TEMPERATE & HILLY. MID TO
HIGH-RISE. INCR LAND VALUE.

SAVANNAH: 1,321 PPL/SQ.MI
HOT & HUMID. HISTORIC. CHEAP
LAND. CONTROLLED ZONING.

Your cultural background has an affect on what density you grow up being comfortable with.

Sociopetal

—WHEN SPACES, BUILDINGS, ROOMS, & FURNITURE ARE DESIGNED TO BRING PEOPLE TOGETHER.

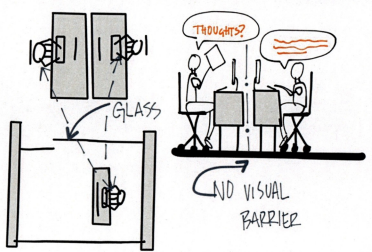

Sociopetal spaces bring people together and allow/promote interaction and collaboration.

Sociofugal

—WHEN SPACES, BUILDINGS, ROOMS, & FURNITURE DISCOURAGE INTERACTION & SOCIAL CONTACT.

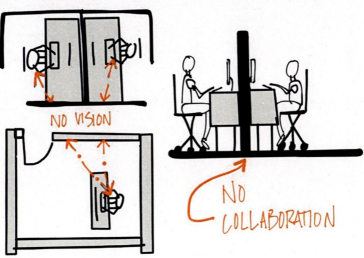

NO VISION

NO COLLABORATION

Sociofugal spaces discourage interaction either intentionally or with poor design.

TERRITORIALITY

A PERSON'S DESIRE TO CALL A PLACE
THEIR OWN.
(READ: WHY UNASSIGNED DESKS IN OPEN
OFFICES SOMETIMES DON'T WORK)

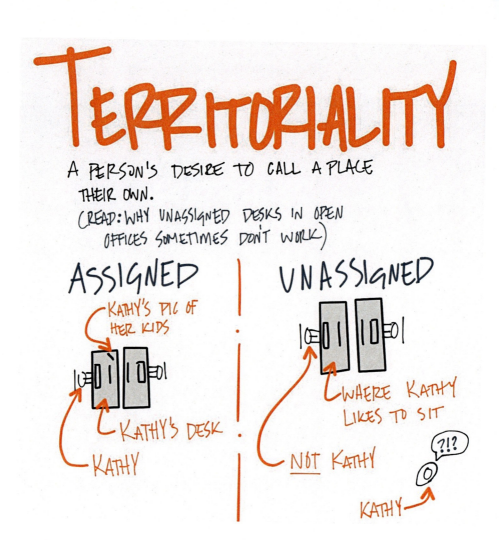

ASSIGNED

KATHY'S PIC OF HER KIDS

KATHY'S DESK

KATHY

UNASSIGNED

WHERE KATHY LIKES TO SIT

NOT KATHY

?!?

KATHY

Everyone wants a place to call their own. The design world calls this "territoriality".

TERRITORIALITY
Subtle + Non-subtle

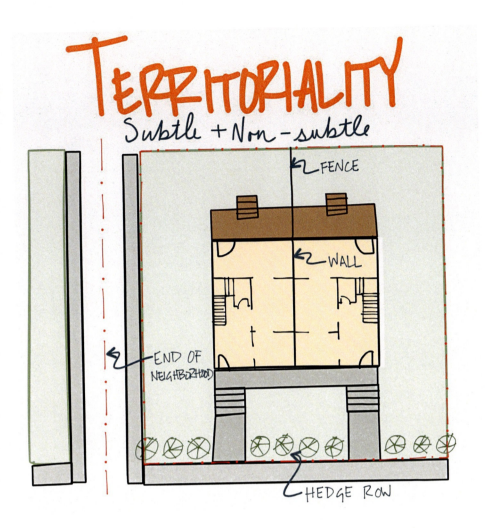

There are subtle and non-subtle aspects of territoriality.

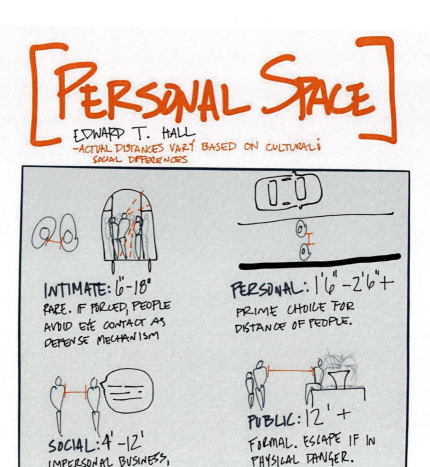

[PERSONAL SPACE]

EDWARD T. HALL
-ACTUAL DISTANCES VARY BASED ON CULTURAL &
SOCIAL DIFFERENCES

INTIMATE: 6"-18"
RARE. IF FORCED, PEOPLE
AVOID EYE CONTACT AS
DEFENSE MECHANISM

PERSONAL: 1'6"-2'6"+
PRIME CHOICE FOR
DISTANCE OF PEOPLE.

SOCIAL: 4'-12'
IMPERSONAL BUSINESS,
WORK, ETC

PUBLIC: 12'+
FORMAL. ESCAPE IF IN
PHYSICAL DANGER.

The actual space distance of personal spaces
varies by culture, but some typical distances are
listed above.

Diversity
≠ SUBURBIA

"THE HUMAN ANIMAL NEEDS A DIVERSE AND STIMULATING ENVIRONMENT. IN A MONOTONOUS URBAN ENVIRONMENT SETTING, COMMUNITY, OR BUILDING, PEOPLE TEND TO BECOME DEPRESSED, IRRITATED, OR SUFFER SOME OTHER TYPE OF NEGATIVE INFLUENCE. OVER A LONG TIME, LIVING IN A DULL, NONSTIMULATING ENVIRONMENT CAN EVEN AFFECT PERSONALITY DEVELOPMENT."

Diversity is important...and it's rarely found in the suburbs.

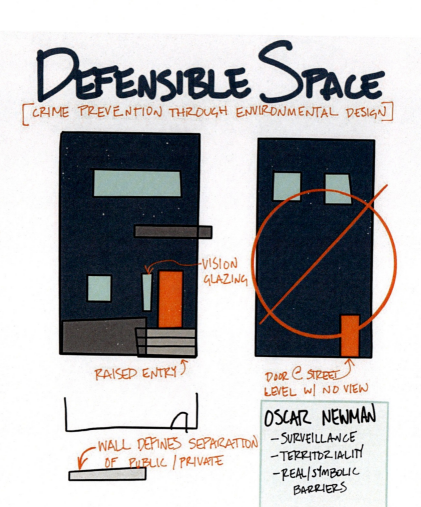

DEFENSIBLE SPACE

[CRIME PREVENTION THROUGH ENVIRONMENTAL DESIGN]

VISION GLAZING

RAISED ENTRY

DOOR @ STREET LEVEL W/ NO VIEW

WALL DEFINES SEPARATION OF PUBLIC / PRIVATE

OSCAR NEWMAN
- SURVEILLANCE
- TERRITORIALITY
- REAL/SYMBOLIC BARRIERS

Weaving together defensible space and sociopetal space isn't easy, but they're both important.

Catchment Areas

- SURROUNDING AREA POPULATION FEEDS AS BASE FOR BUSINESSES, SCHOOLS, ETC

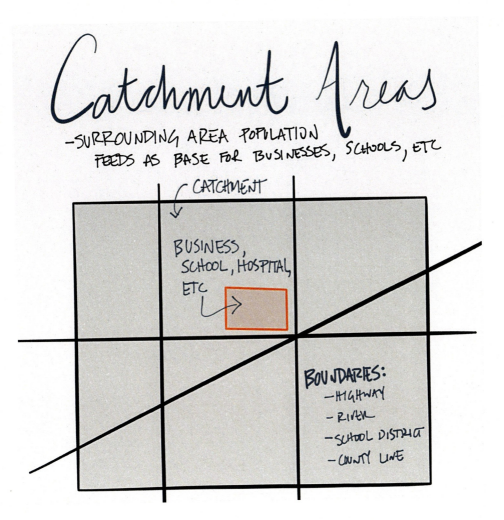

CATCHMENT

BUSINESS, SCHOOL, HOSPITAL, ETC

BOUNDARIES:
- HIGHWAY
- RIVER
- SCHOOL DISTRICT
- COUNTY LINE

The catchment area feeds local businesses, schools, and stores.

ACCESSIBILITY TO TRANSPORTATION

– CRITICAL TO SITE SELECTION / DEVELOPMENT

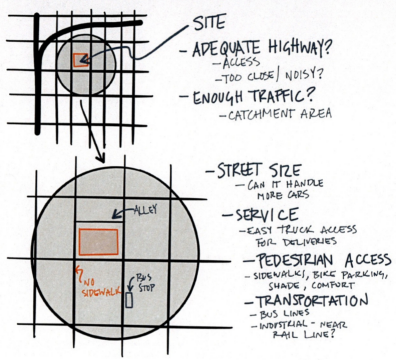

SITE
- ADEQUATE HIGHWAY?
  – ACCESS
  – TOO CLOSE / NOISY?
- ENOUGH TRAFFIC?
  – CATCHMENT AREA

– STREET SIZE
  – CAN IT HANDLE MORE CARS
– SERVICE
  – EASY TRUCK ACCESS FOR DELIVERIES
– PEDESTRIAN ACCESS
  – SIDEWALKS, BIKE PARKING, SHADE, COMFORT
– TRANSPORTATION
  – BUS LINES
  – INDUSTRIAL – NEAR RAIL LINE?

ALLEY

NO SIDEWALK

BUS STOP

Many design features affect accessibility to transportation. Note: it's not all about cars.

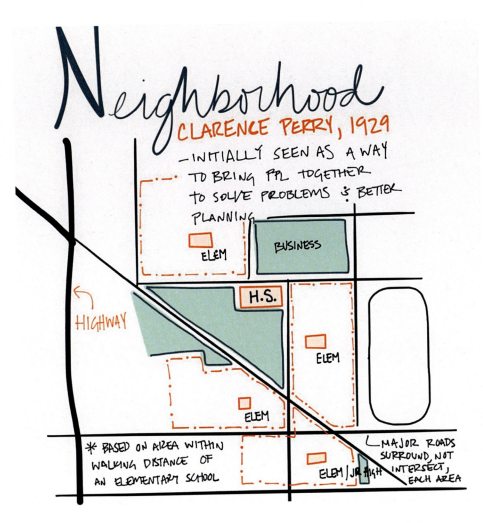

Neighborhood

CLARENCE PERRY, 1929

— INITIALLY SEEN AS A WAY TO BRING PPL TOGETHER TO SOLVE PROBLEMS & BETTER PLANNING

ELEM

BUSINESS

H.S.

HIGHWAY

ELEM

ELEM

* BASED ON AREA WITHIN WALKING DISTANCE OF AN ELEMENTARY SCHOOL

ELEM | JR HIGH

└ MAJOR ROADS SURROUND, NOT INTERSECT, EACH AREA

The idea of the walkable neighborhood and its needs were theorized by Clarence Perry in the early 1900s.

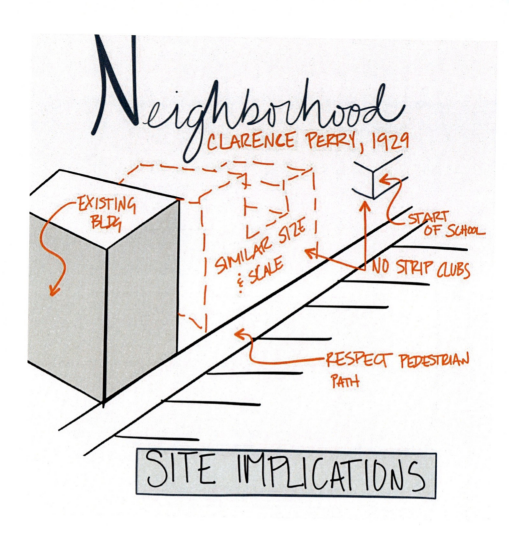

Neighborhood
CLARENCE PERRY, 1929

EXISTING BLDG

SIMILAR SIZE & SCALE

START OF SCHOOL

NO STRIP CLUBS

RESPECT PEDESTRIAN PATH

SITE IMPLICATIONS

There are a variety of important site implications to consider when designing within a neighborhood.

For a neighborhood to thrive, public interest locations have to be programmed into the planning.

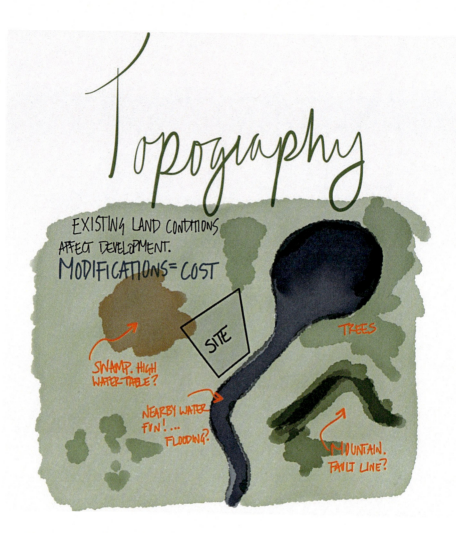

Topography plays an important role in planning a site and building program.

TOPOGRAPHIC MAP

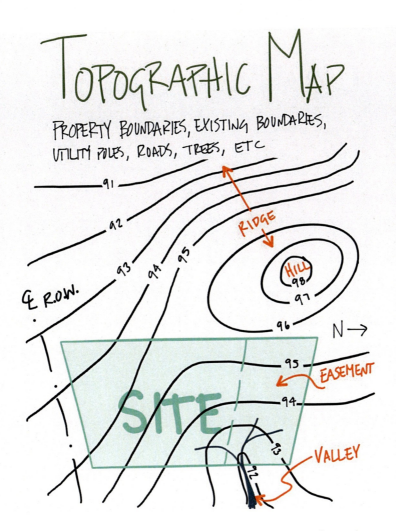

PROPERTY BOUNDARIES, EXISTING BOUNDARIES, UTILITY POLES, ROADS, TREES, ETC

91
92
93 94 95
₵ R.O.W.
RIDGE
HILL 98
97
96
N →
95
EASEMENT
94
SITE
93
92
VALLEY

A topographic map will show utilities, legal boundaries, roads, major land changes, etc.

Contour Lines

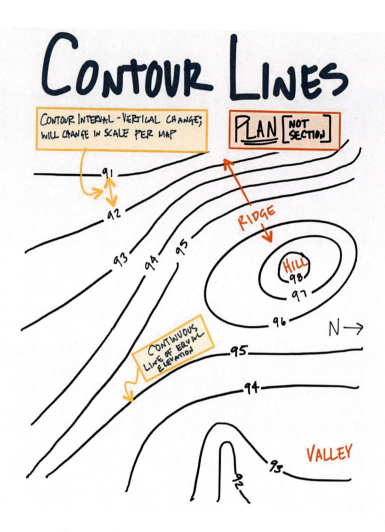

CONTOUR INTERVAL – VERTICAL CHANGE; WILL CHANGE IN SCALE PER MAP

PLAN [NOT SECTION]

91

92

93 94 95

RIDGE

HILL 98

97

96

N →

CONTINUOUS LINE OF EQUAL ELEVATION

95

94

93

92

VALLEY

Contour lines show elevation change in plan. Proximity shows slope and major land features like ridges and valleys.

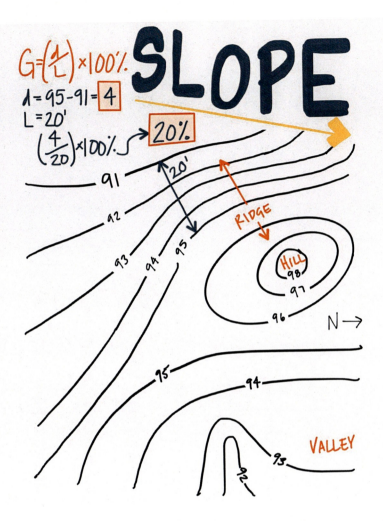

$G = \left(\dfrac{1}{L}\right) \times 100\%$

$1 = 95 - 91 = \boxed{4}$

$L = 20'$

$\left(\dfrac{4}{20}\right) \times 100\% \rightarrow \boxed{20\%}$

SLOPE

91
92
93   94   95
20'

RIDGE

HILL
98
97
96   N →

95
94

VALLEY
93
92

Slope is the vertical change over the horizontal length. There are minimums and maximums depending on use.

Slope Design

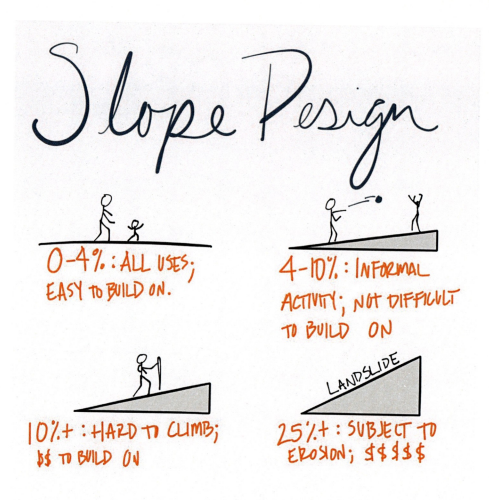

0-4% : ALL USES; EASY TO BUILD ON.

4-10% : INFORMAL ACTIVITY; NOT DIFFICULT TO BUILD ON

10%+ : HARD TO CLIMB; $$ TO BUILD ON

LANDSLIDE

25%+ : SUBJECT TO EROSION; $$$$

Certain slopes allow or are better suited for different types of use. Other slopes should be avoided entirely.

SITE SECTION

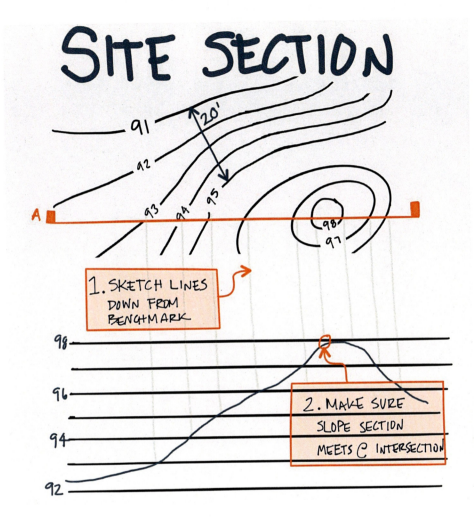

91
20'
92
93 94 95
A
98
97

1. SKETCH LINES
DOWN FROM
BENCHMARK

98
96
94
92

2. MAKE SURE
SLOPE SECTION
MEETS @ INTERSECTION

Knowing how to read and prepare a site section is important, both for the ARE and your work as a professional.

SITE FEATURES

— ALSO CHECK FOR SUBSURFACE WATER
& ROCK

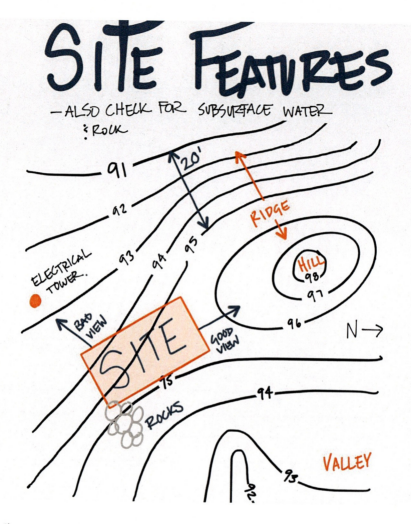

Views, water, major land features, utilities, etc should all be taken into account when locating a site.

Drainage

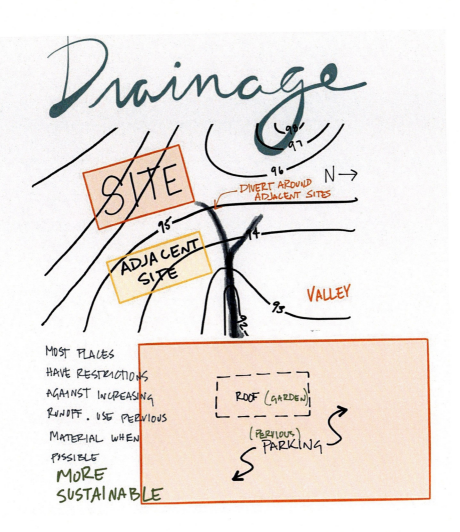

SITE

98
97
96
95
94
93
92

N →

DIVERT AROUND ADJACENT SITES

ADJACENT SITE

VALLEY

MOST PLACES HAVE RESTRICTIONS AGAINST INCREASING RUNOFF. USE PERVIOUS MATERIAL WHEN PISSIBLE
MORE SUSTAINABLE

ROOF (GARDEN)

(PERVIOUS) PARKING

Water and gravity will most always work against you. Design and plan for them.

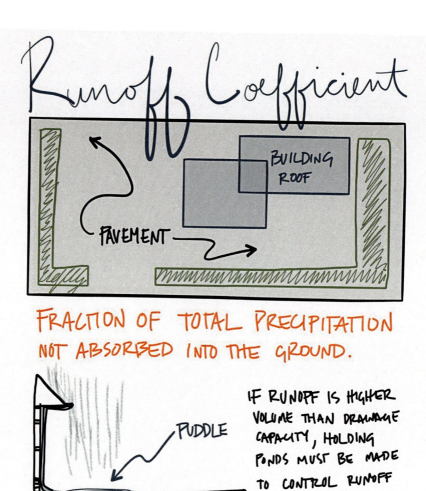

Runoff Coefficient

BUILDING ROOF

PAVEMENT

FRACTION OF TOTAL PRECIPITATION NOT ABSORBED INTO THE GROUND.

PUDDLE

IF RUNOFF IS HIGHER VOLUME THAN DRAINAGE CAPACITY, HOLDING PONDS MUST BE MADE TO CONTROL RUNOFF

The effects of stress on the stormwater system determine site design and ability to achieve sustainable initiatives.

SILT FENCE

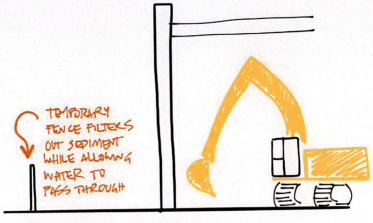

TEMPORARY FENCE FILTERS OUT SEDIMENT WHILE ALLOWING WATER TO PASS THROUGH

- GEO TEXTILE FABRIC
- PLACED @ PERIMETER OF CONSTRUCTION SITE

Silt fences are integral to the construction process. (building in background, machine in foreground)

Soil

TOPSOIL -
MINERAL + ORGANIC
FEW INCHES TO 1' + DEEP
(PEAT, SILT, CLAY, LOAM)

MINERAL -
MOSTLY MINERAL, SOME
FRACTURED ROCK.
(GRAVEL, SAND, CLAY)

BEDROCK -
GOOD FOR BEARING,
HARD TO EXCAVATE

Until we start building underwater or in the sky, soil is the main grounding force we need to understand.

Soil Types

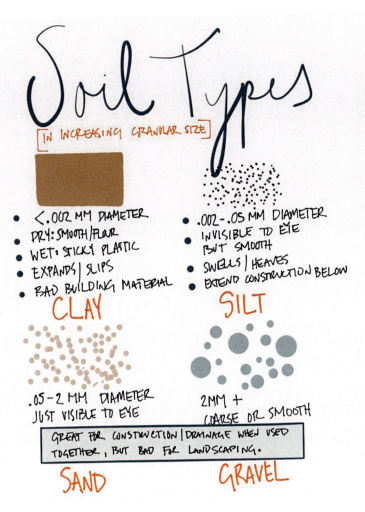

- < .002 MM DIAMETER
- DRY: SMOOTH/FLOUR
- WET: STICKY PLASTIC
- EXPANDS / SLIPS
- BAD BUILDING MATERIAL

CLAY

- .002 - .05 MM DIAMETER
- INVISIBLE TO EYE BUT SMOOTH
- SWELLS / HEAVES
- EXTEND CONSTRUCTION BELOW

SILT

.05 - 2 MM DIAMETER
JUST VISIBLE TO EYE

2MM +
COARSE OR SMOOTH

GREAT FOR CONSTRUCTION / DRAINAGE WHEN USED TOGETHER, BUT BAD FOR LANDSCAPING.

SAND

GRAVEL

Soil size, style, and structural ability are all important to understand and important for the structural stability of your design. Some soils should be avoided.

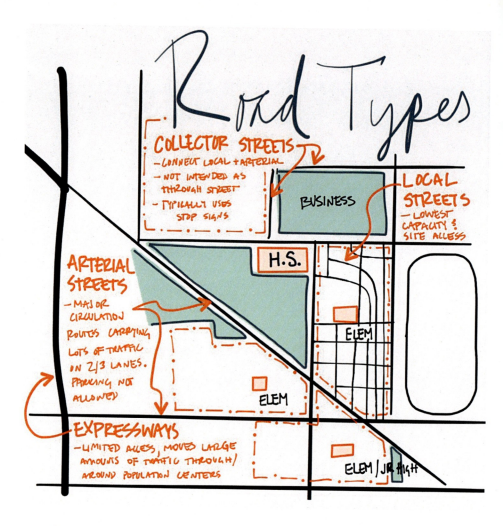

There are 4 types of roadways that make up our transit: Local, Collector, Arterial, and Expressway.

ROAD LAYOUTS

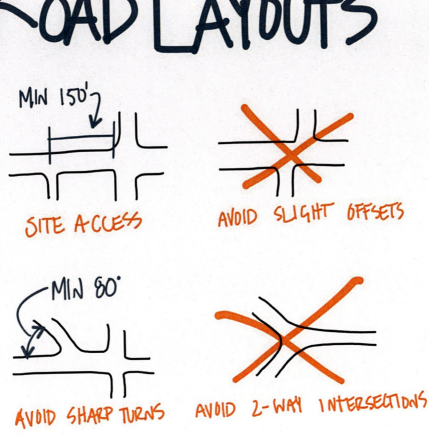

MIN 150'

SITE ACCESS

AVOID SLIGHT OFFSETS

MIN 80°

AVOID SHARP TURNS

AVOID 2-WAY INTERSECTIONS

Road layouts affect the efficiency and safety of your site.

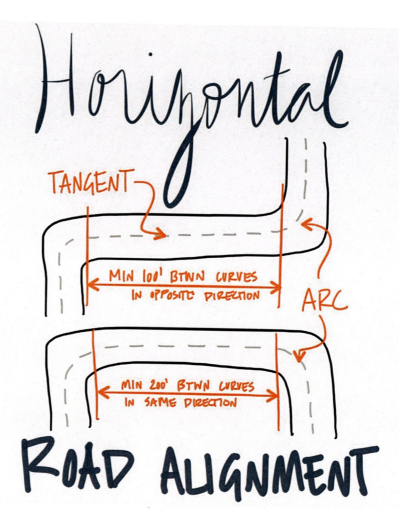

Horizontal

TANGENT

MIN 100' BTWN CURVES
IN OPPOSITE DIRECTION

ARC

MIN 200' BTWN CURVES
IN SAME DIRECTION

ROAD ALIGNMENT

There are minimum travel distances to be aware of for road layouts.

Vertical

SMOOTH TRANSITION

MAX 10%

[RULE OF THUMB]

ROAD ALIGNMENT

Winding hills may be fun to drive on, but you should be aware of grades and transitions.

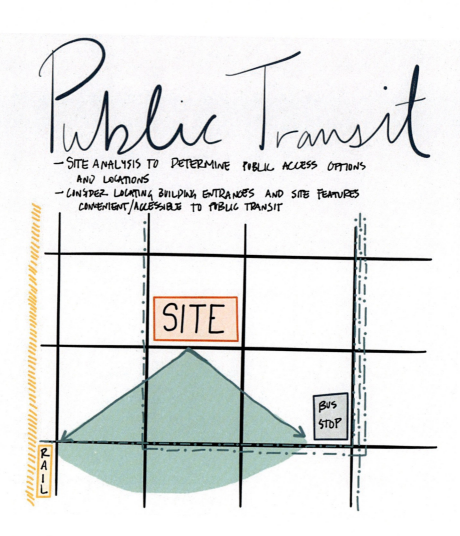

Public transit access is an important option to consider (and try to design for).

UTILITIES

SANITARY & STORM SEWERS TAKE PRIORITY BECAUSE OF GRAVITY.

RIGHT-OF-WAY

PROPOSED BUILDING

1 MI

EXPENSIVE TO RUN BUILDING WATER MAIN THIS FAR

EXISTING BUILDING

ELEC & TCOM

GAS

WATER

SHORT DISTANCE

Knowing how and where utilities typically get run is important.

MUNICIPAL ACCESS

—FIRE, POLICE, STREET CLEANING, SNOW REMOVAL, TRASH REMOVAL

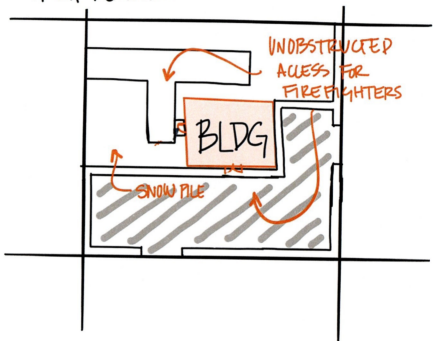

Municipal access is important and in some cases (fire lanes) mandated.

SERVICE ACCESS

*NOT POSSIBLE IN URBAN/INFILL SETTINGS
- KEEP AUTO/PEDESTRIAN AND SERVICE SEPARATE
- TYPICALLY SPECIFIED BY LOCAL ZONING CODES

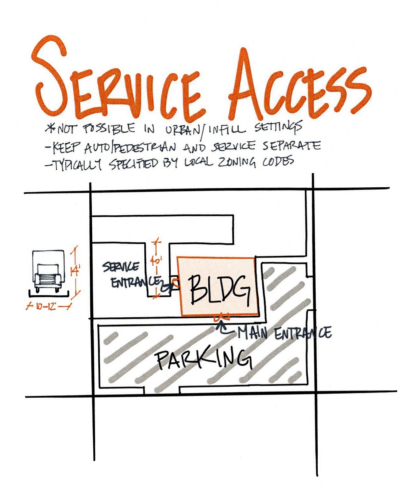

Sometimes in urban infill projects, on-site service access is impossible. There are minimum turn-around radius and extension requirements.

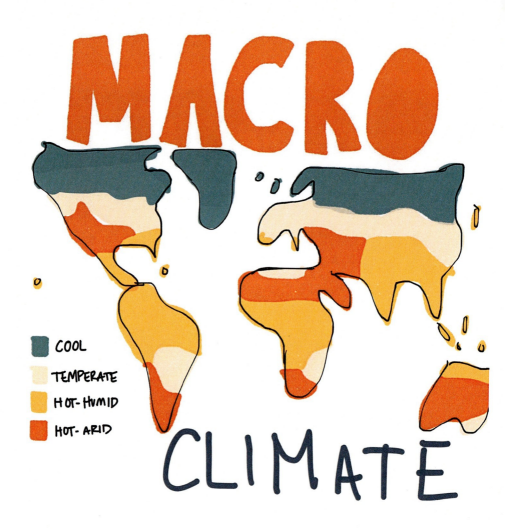

MACRO

CLIMATE

- COOL
- TEMPERATE
- HOT-HUMID
- HOT-ARID

Macroclimates are the first piece of weather that affects your site climate.

MICRO

SITE-SPECIFIC MODIFICATION AFFECTS MICROCLIMATE

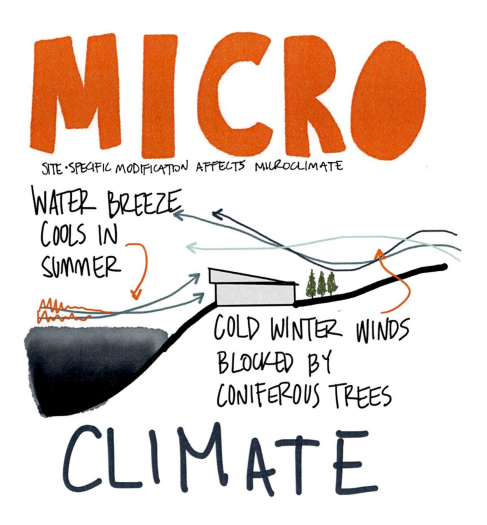

WATER BREEZE
COOLS IN
SUMMER

COLD WINTER WINDS
BLOCKED BY
CONIFEROUS TREES

CLIMATE

A microclimate is created with on-site conditions and design choices.

Wind Patterns

PREVAILING PATTERNS & MICROCLIMATE EFFECTS SHOULD BE STUDIED

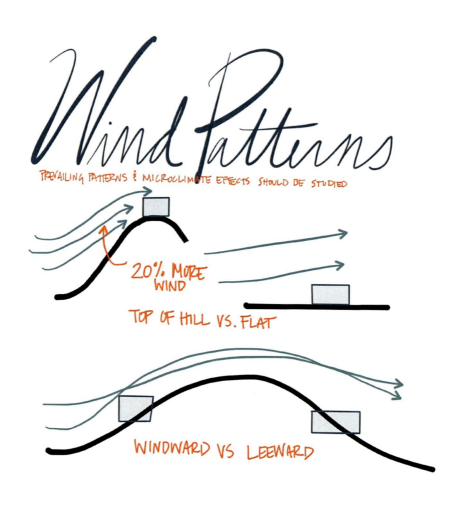

20% MORE WIND

TOP OF HILL VS. FLAT

WINDWARD VS LEEWARD

Wind patterns will affect your microclimate. Building placement on the site will help or hurt this perceived comfort (or lack thereof).

80

Water & Wind

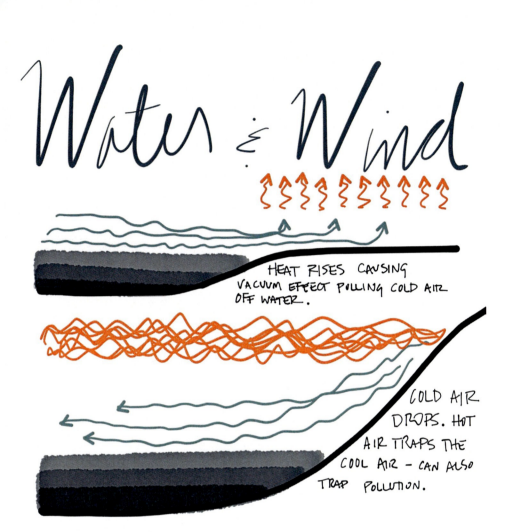

HEAT RISES CAUSING VACUUM EFFECT PULLING COLD AIR OFF WATER.

COLD AIR DROPS. HOT AIR TRAPS THE COOL AIR — CAN ALSO TRAP POLLUTION.

Water will affect your microclimate. Use it to your advantage (everyone loves water when it's not coming through their roof).

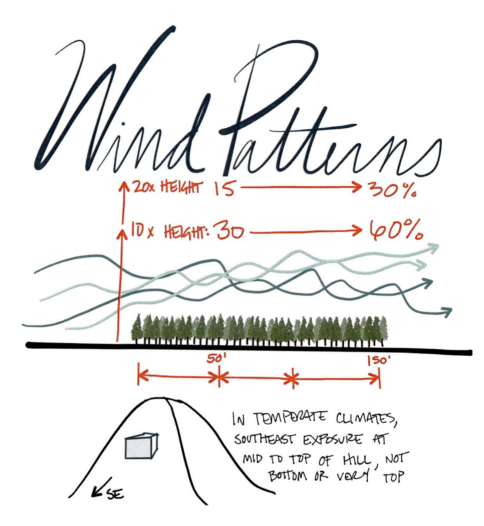

Wind Patterns

20x HEIGHT 15 ⟶ 30%

10x HEIGHT: 30 ⟶ 60%

50'   150'

IN TEMPERATE CLIMATES, SOUTHEAST EXPOSURE AT MID TO TOP OF HILL, NOT BOTTOM OR VERY TOP

SE

Wind at different heights off the ground can be reduced by man-made blockades or rows of trees.

SOLAR ORIENTATION

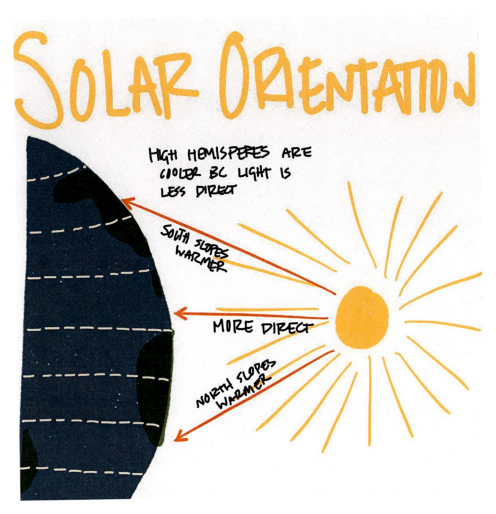

Solar orientation affects the microclimate. Sun can be your friend if you use it properly.

Understanding albedo will take you far in human comfort and sustainable design (and client happiness).

CONDUCTIVITY

TIME RATE OF FLOW OF HEAT THRU MATERIAL

HIGHLY CONDUCTIVE

METAL

CONCRETE & MASONRY

LOW CONDUCTIVITY

NATURAL MATERIALS

ALSO WOOD, WOOL,
FIBER-GLASS...
(THINK INSULATION)

Conductivity and thermal breaks. Your friend or the bane of your existence.

ALBEDO + CONDUCTIVITY

[AFFECT MICROCLIMATE]

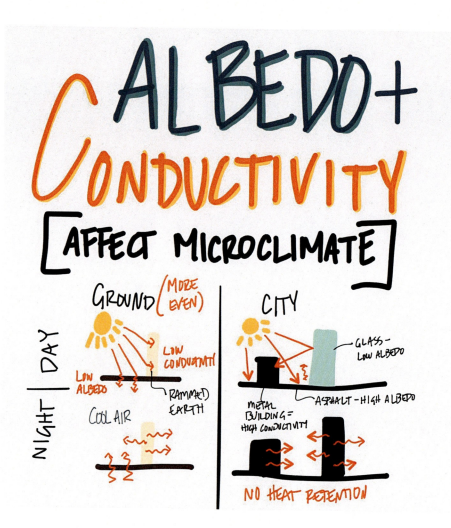

Know how albedo and conductivity work together or against each other.

SUSTAINABLE

FULL LIFE CYCLE OF ENVIRONMENTAL IMPACT

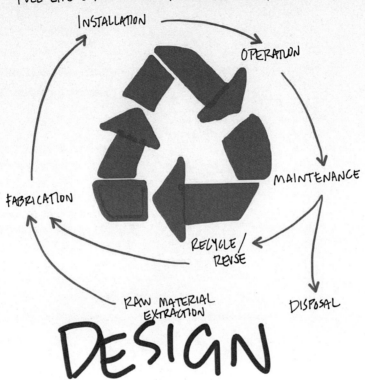

INSTALLATION

OPERATION

MAINTENANCE

FABRICATION

RECYCLE/ REUSE

RAW MATERIAL EXTRACTION

DISPOSAL

DESIGN

Sustainability: it is (or should be) a part of every design thought and decision.

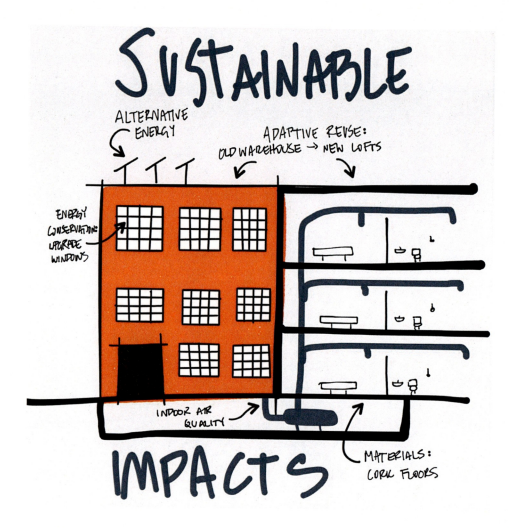

Above are some of the core subjects of sustainability affecting design.

ECOLOGY OF

[ENFORCED BY EPA]

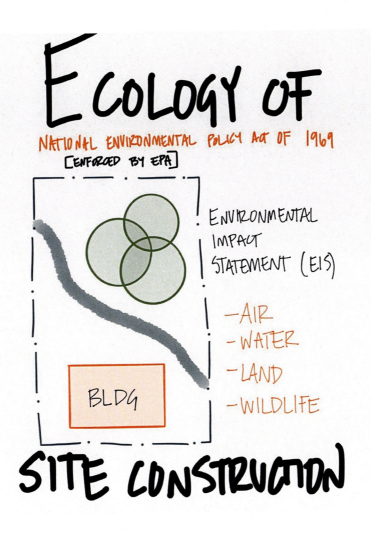

ENVIRONMENTAL
IMPACT
STATEMENT (EIS)

−AIR
−WATER
−LAND
−WILDLIFE

BLDG

SITE CONSTRUCTION

We don't build underwater or in space yet...we build on land. That means we affect the ecology of a site.

Wetland

AREA WHOSE SOIL IS INUNDATED OR SATURATED
WITH SURFACE WATER OR GROUND WATER
FREQUENTLY ENOUGH THAT IT CAN SUPPORT
PLANTS NEEDING SATURATED SOIL.

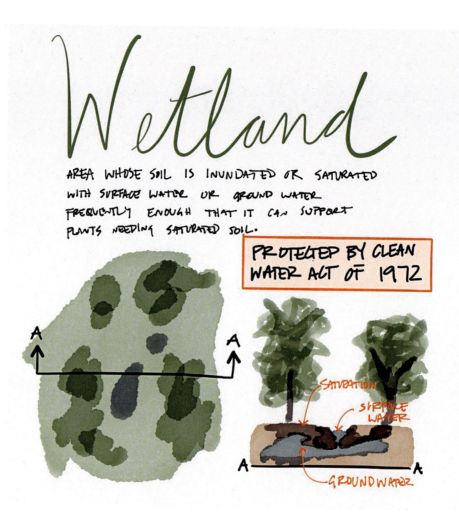

PROTECTED BY CLEAN
WATER ACT OF 1972

A — A

SATURATION

SURFACE
WATER

A — A

GROUND WATER

Wetlands are protected. Repeat after me: wetlands. are. protected. That's all you have to remember about them.

SUSTAINABLE

▨ = NO CONSTRUCTION

PRIME FARMLAND

ENDANGERED SPECIES HABITAT

HISTORIC SITE

5' ELEVATION WITHIN 100 YR. FLOODPLAIN

100' WITHIN WETLAND

SITE SELECTION

Wetlands, farmlands, historic sites, endangered species, floodplains...know how they affect site selection.

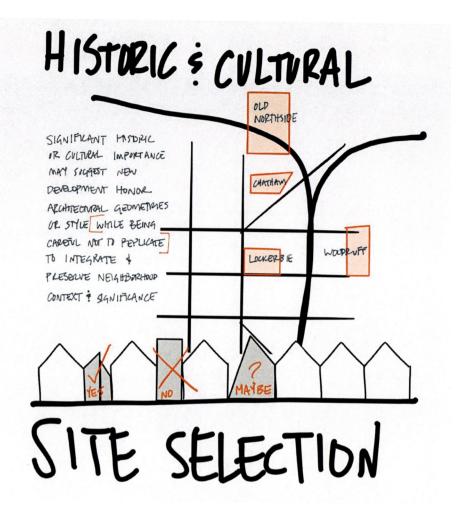

SITE SELECTION

Know your context. Historic areas may cause zoning restrictions and affect site selection for your project type.

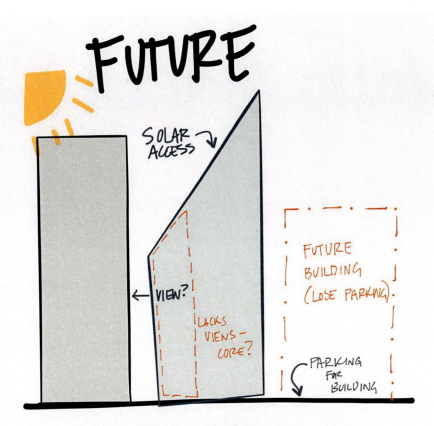

The sun is nice, but you have to think about solar access in context.

AIR & GROUND

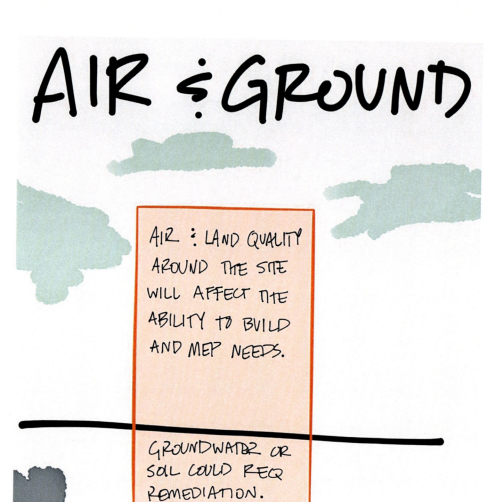

AIR & LAND QUALITY AROUND THE SITE WILL AFFECT THE ABILITY TO BUILD AND MEP NEEDS.

GROUNDWATER OR SOIL COULD REQ REMEDIATION.

Air and land affect the built environment. And the built environment affects them. There are sustainable considerations outside of your building.

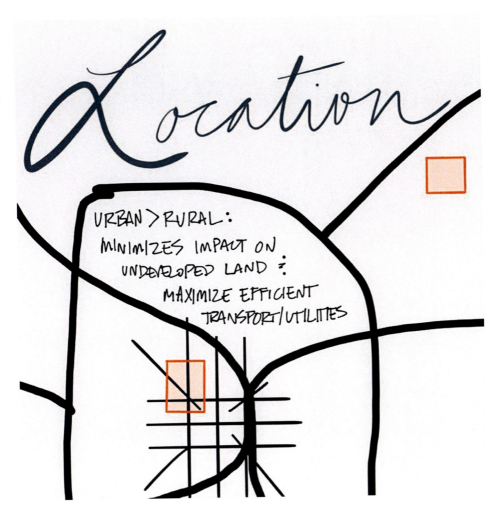

Location

URBAN > RURAL:
MINIMIZES IMPACT ON
UNDEVELOPED LAND ∴
MAXIMIZE EFFICIENT
TRANSPORT/UTILITIES

Think about the impact of new development vs REdevelopment.

MIXED USE

MANY OPTIONS OF MIXED-USE BUILDINGS GIVE PEOPLE THE OPTION TO LIVE, WORK, AND PLAY IN THE COMMUNITY.

Mixed use helps you live locally (if done right).

LOCATION

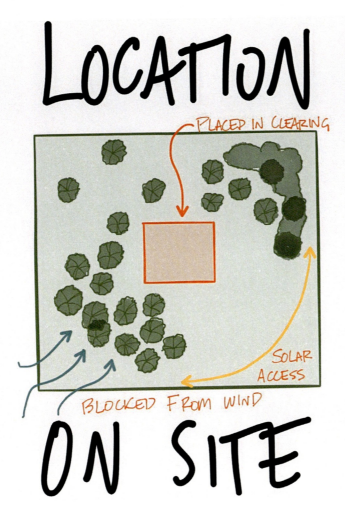

ON SITE

There are many things to consider with building placement. Sustainability is one.

SOLAR SHADOWS

SHARE THE SUN

Light issues as NYC grew created zoning for setbacks to share the sun. Now most cities have implemented setbacks related to their scale.

Wind is an important factor in building massing and design.

BUILDING FOOTPRINT

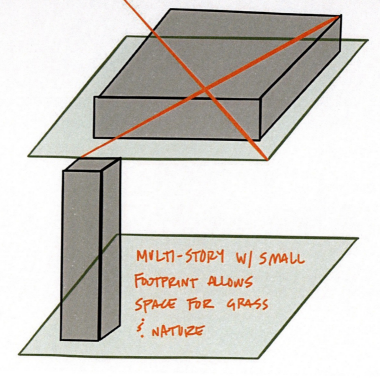

MULTI-STORY W/ SMALL FOOTPRINT ALLOWS SPACE FOR GRASS & NATURE

When building sustainably, typically there's less footprint.

MATERIAL DIMENSIONS

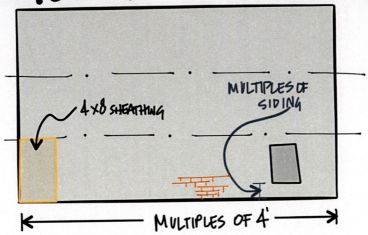

4×8 SHEATHING

MULTIPLES OF SIDING

|← MULTIPLES OF 4' →|

REDUCE WASTE BY KNOWING TYP. DIMENSIONS OF MATERIALS AND OPTIMIZING BUILDING DESIGN. CUSTOM DIMENSIONS MEAN $$$ AND WASTED MATERIALS.

What are buildings made of? Materials. Plan wisely - it affects sustainability.

Roofing

EFFECT ON TEMPERATURE

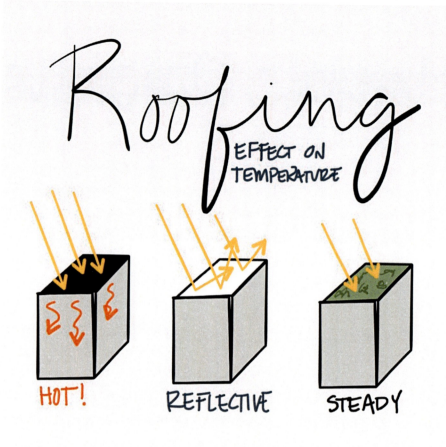

HOT!　　　REFLECTIVE　　　STEADY

The material and coloring of roofing affects the heat/cool load on a building.

SITE DISTURBANCE

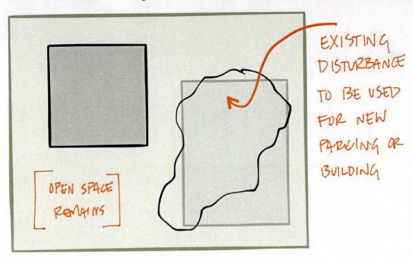

EXISTING DISTURBANCE TO BE USED FOR NEW PARKING OR BUILDING

OPEN SPACE REMAINS

Building on a previously disturbed site lets green space (undisturbed) ecosystems that might have otherwise been used stay intact.

EARTHWORK

IT'S EXPENSIVE. PLAN TO USE SITE OR SLOPE TO ADVANTAGE.

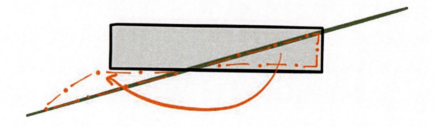

That dirt is expensive. Plan ahead.

UTILITY CORRIDORS

PLAN TO USE PREVIOUSLY DEVELOPED SPACE ON SITE OR NEW ROAD/WALKWAYS FOR UTILITIES. LESS SITE DISTURBANCE DURING CONSTRUCTION AND FUTURE MAINTENANCE..

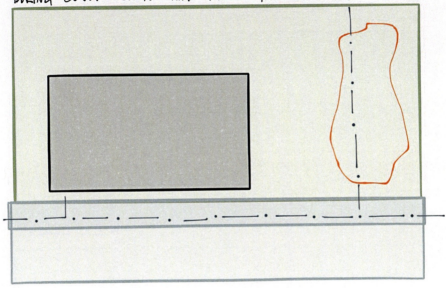

Utility connections aren't cheap, especially not a retrofit. Plan for these early in design.

SITE DISTURBANCE

LIMIT SITE DISTURBANCE TO MINIMIZE IMPACT.

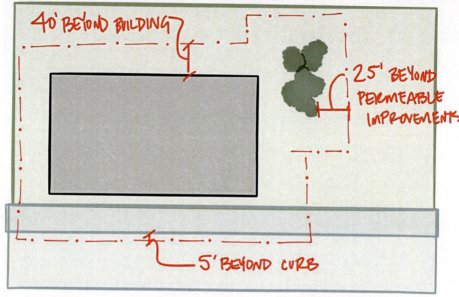

40' BEYOND BUILDING

25' BEYOND PERMEABLE IMPROVEMENTS

5' BEYOND CURB

IF YOU'RE IN AN URBAN SETTING, YOU SHOULD DO YOUR BEST TO KEEP THE SIDEWALK OPEN.

The less you disturb, the less that has to try to regrow (or fauna that gets displaced).

PARKING

MORE $$$
BUT BETTER
FOR ENVIRONMENT

If sustainability is your focus (and you have no budget issues) put your parking in the vertical plane and give the ground space back to the environment. It's all about footprint.

HEAT ISLAND

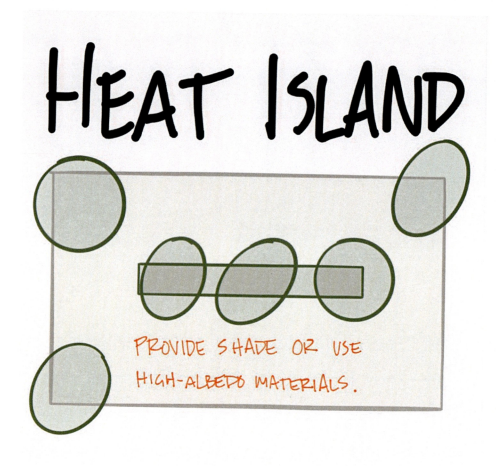

PROVIDE SHADE OR USE
HIGH-ALBEDO MATERIALS.

Heat island effect is a big deal. Understand the concepts to counter or prevent it at every chance.

PERVIOUS PAVING

PERVIOUS PAVING REDUCES THE STRESS ON STORMWATER SYSTEMS.

Pervious paving has a higher upfront cost, but a lot of positives on the backend.

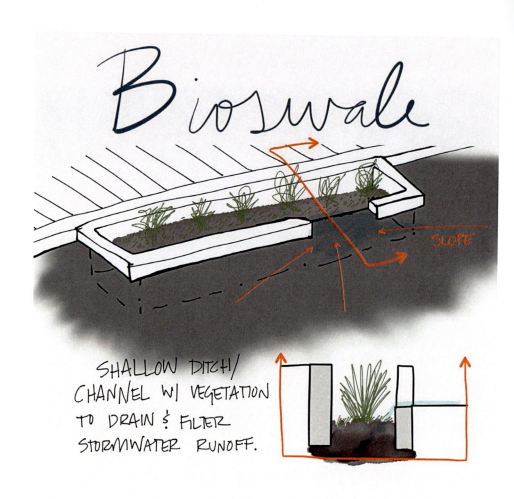

Bioswale

SHALLOW DITCH/ CHANNEL W/ VEGETATION TO DRAIN & FILTER STORMWATER RUNOFF.

SLOPE

Bioswales act as a natural stormwater filter to reduce the potential overload on a stormwater sewer system.

Site Lighting

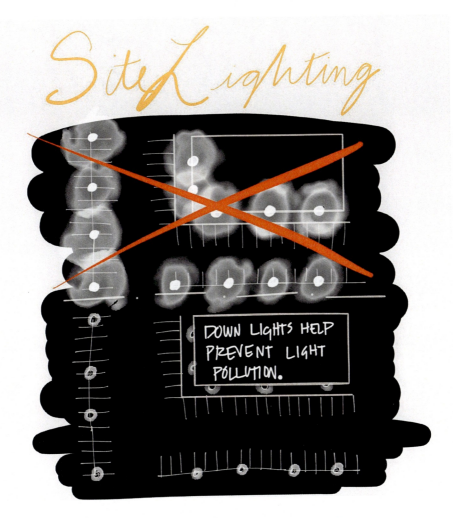

Design to help prevent or minimize light pollution. Understand how and why it's bad.

RAINWATER

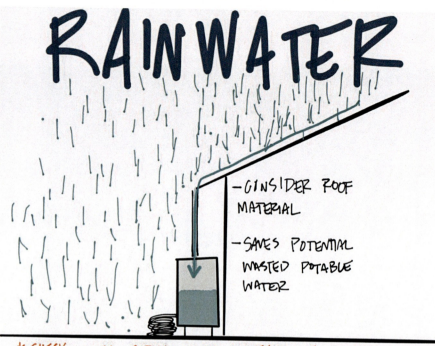

- CONSIDER ROOF MATERIAL

- SAVES POTENTIAL WASTED POTABLE WATER

*CHECK LOCAL CODES: IT IS ILLEGAL IN SOME PLACES TO HARVEST RAINWATER

COLLECTION

Rainwater collection reduces the impact on the potable water supply by diverting it for things like irrigation or other non-potable uses. (Potable = drinkable)

Native Plants

PLANT / INSECT HABITAT

NATIVE PLANTS / MEADOWS PREVENT IRRIGATION NEEDS FROM MANICURED LAWNS.

MINIMIZE IMPERVIOUS SPACE.

Consider the long-term effects of planting types.

1916 ZONING

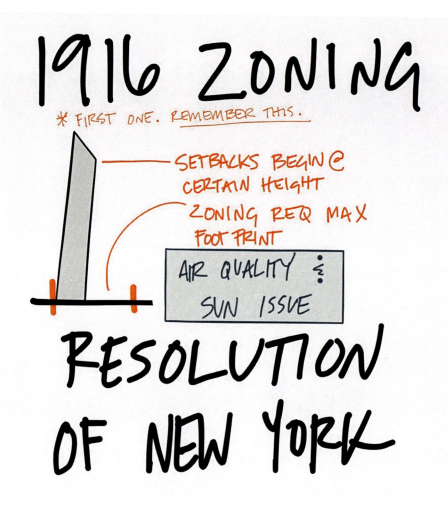

* FIRST ONE. REMEMBER THIS.

SETBACKS BEGIN @ CERTAIN HEIGHT

ZONING REQ MAX FOOT PRINT

AIR QUALITY & SUN ISSUE

RESOLUTION OF NEW YORK

The first zoning law was in 1916 in NYC.
REMEMBER THIS.

SITE ZONING

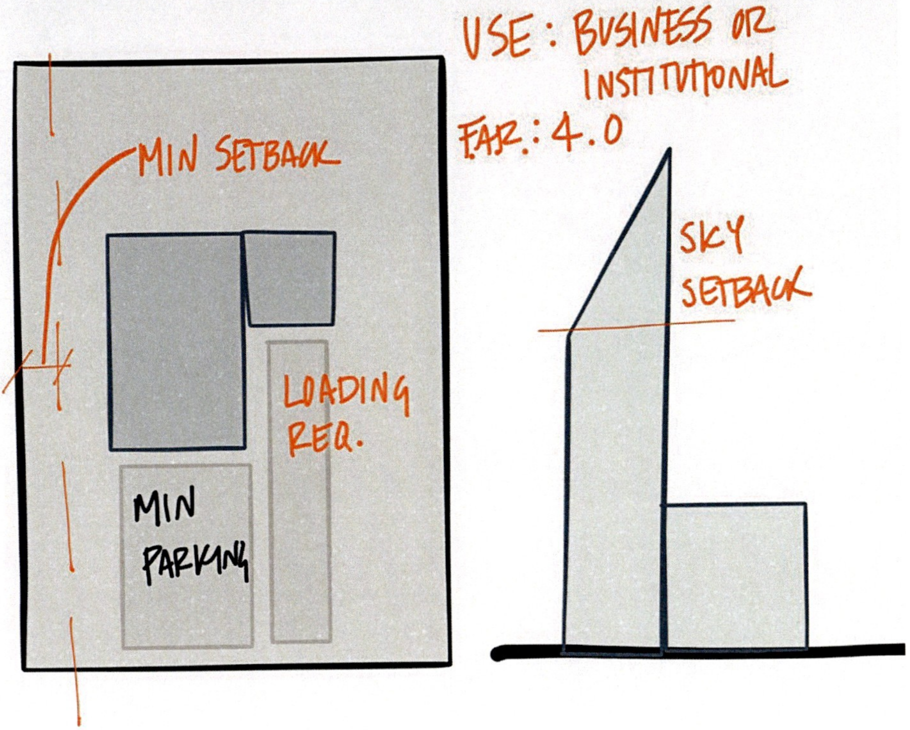

USE: BUSINESS OR INSTITUTIONAL

FAR: 4.0

MIN SETBACK

LOADING REQ.

MIN PARKING

SKY SETBACK

Site zoning laws affect the overall programmatic shape of a building.

Zoning 101

DIVISION OF CITY INTO DISTRICTS

LEARN

ART

BIZ

BUILD

REGULATES:
- LAND USE
- BUILDING SIZE
- LOCATION ON PROPERTY / IN DISTRICT

LEGAL BASIS: PROTECT HEALTH, SAFETY, WELFARE OF CITIZENS

The intention of zoning is to protect the health, safety, and welfare of citizens.

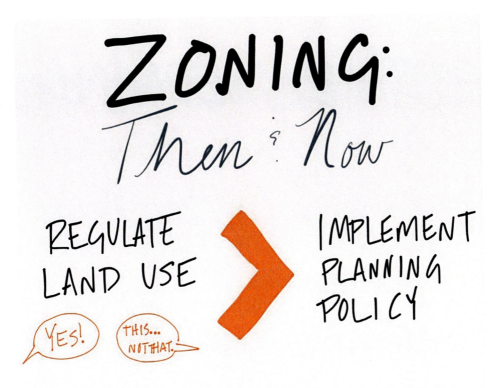

Zoning has adapted from it's initial power of prescriptive rules to planning policy implementation.

OTHER ZONING

1 SIGNAGE & WAYFINDING REQUIREMENTS

2 RURAL ZONING

    — SEPARATE AGRICULTURE FROM
        FOREST 2

3 FLOODPLAIN ZONING

4 AIRPORT ZONING

5 HISTORIC AREA ZONING 4

There are other pieces of zoning that either protect or set aside space for certain uses.

FLOOR AREA RATIO

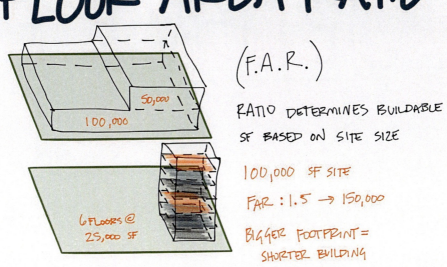

(F.A.R.)

RATIO DETERMINES BUILDABLE
SF BASED ON SITE SIZE

100,000 SF SITE
FAR : 1.5 → 150,000
BIGGER FOOTPRINT =
    SHORTER BUILDING

50,000

100,000

6 FLOORS @
25,000 SF

Floor Area Ratio (FAR) affects your square footage allowance on a site. What you do with it is up to you.

SETBACKS

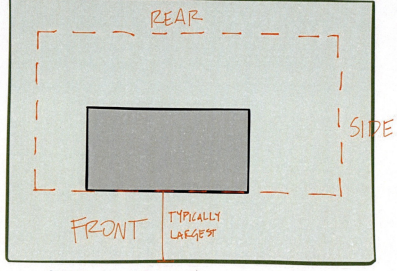

REAR

SIDE

FRONT | TYPICALLY LARGEST

SETBACKS AFFECT THE DESIGNS TO MEET F.A.R.

Setbacks affect how and where you place a building on a site, as well as your ability to meet maximum FAR.

BULK PLANE

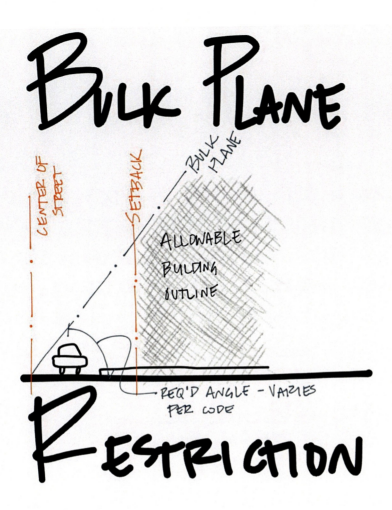

CENTER OF STREET

SETBACK

BULK PLANE

ALLOWABLE
BUILDING
OUTLINE

REQ'D ANGLE - VARIES
PER CODE

RESTRICTION

Zoning + sun = Bulk Plane Restrictions.

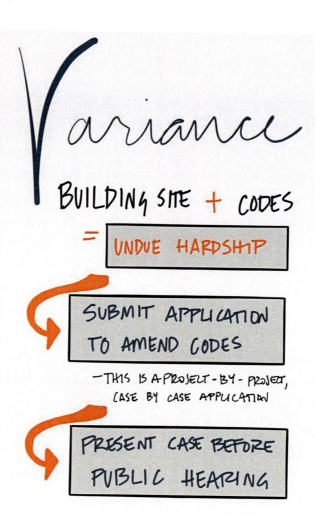

Variance

BUILDING SITE + CODES

= UNDUE HARDSHIP

SUBMIT APPLICATION TO AMEND CODES

—THIS IS A PROJECT-BY-PROJECT, CASE BY CASE APPLICATION

PRESENT CASE BEFORE PUBLIC HEARING

Variances help to relieve the project of "undue hardships".

NONCONFORMING

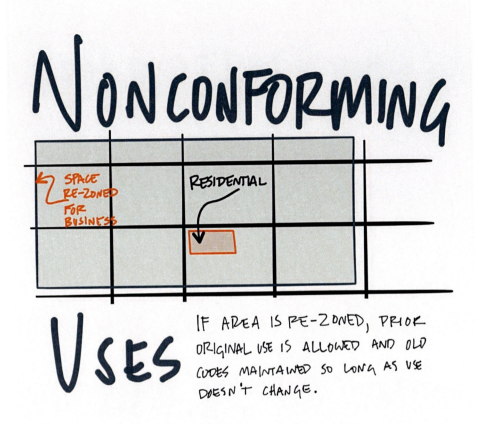

SPACE RE-ZONED FOR BUSINESS

RESIDENTIAL

USES

IF AREA IS RE-ZONED, PRIOR ORIGINAL USE IS ALLOWED AND OLD CODES MAINTAINED SO LONG AS USE DOESN'T CHANGE.

Non-conforming uses are grandfathered in if an area gets re-zoned.

CONDITIONAL

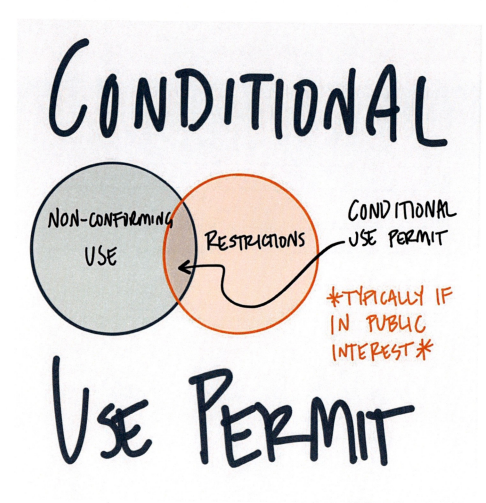

NON-CONFIRMING USE

RESTRICTIONS

CONDITIONAL USE PERMIT

TYPICALLY IF IN PUBLIC INTEREST

USE PERMIT

A conditional use permit is different than a variance in that it typically is in the public interest.

UTILITY

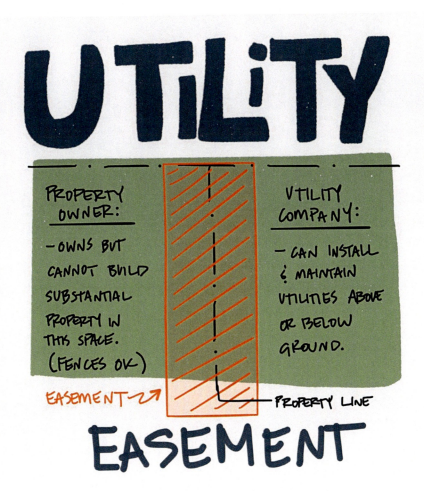

PROPERTY OWNER:

- OWNS BUT CANNOT BUILD SUBSTANTIAL PROPERTY IN THIS SPACE. (FENCES OK)

VTILITY COMPANY:

- CAN INSTALL & MAINTAIN VTILITIES ABOVE OR BELOW GROUND.

EASEMENT ⤳

PROPERTY LINE

EASEMENT

Utility easements allow you to build impermanent things within its area. This means a fence is okay, but a building or foundation for a deck is not.

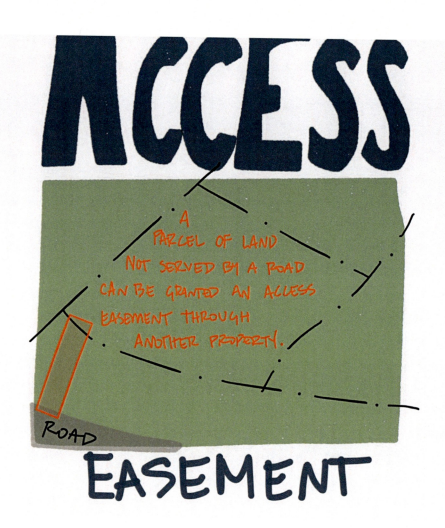

ACCESS

A PARCEL OF LAND NOT SERVED BY A ROAD CAN BE GRANTED AN ACCESS EASEMENT THROUGH ANOTHER PROPERTY.

ROAD

EASEMENT

Access easements are used frequently to connect public land/parks.

OTHER EASEMENTS

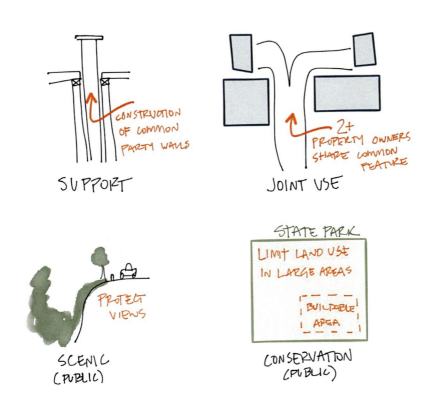

SUPPORT — CONSTRUCTION OF COMMON PARTY WALLS

JOINT USE — 2+ PROPERTY OWNERS SHARE COMMON FEATURE

SCENIC (PUBLIC) — PROTECT VIEWS

CONSERVATION (PUBLIC) — STATE PARK, LIMIT LAND USE IN LARGE AREAS, BUILDABLE AREA

There are a variety of other easements that could affect your site/building.

RESTRICTIVE

- PROVISION IN A DEED
- LEGAL & ENFORCEABLE IF REASONABLE
  AND IN THE PUBLIC INTEREST.
- SETBACKS
- MIN SQUARE FOOTAGE
- MATERIAL TYPES
- ETC

*BE CAREFUL. THIS
CAN LEAD TO DULL
MONOTONY (SUBURBS).

COVENANTS

Restrictive covenants are a part of property legalese.

AFFIRMATIVE

— REQUIRES BUYER TO PERFORM SPECIFIC DUTY AFTER PURCHASE

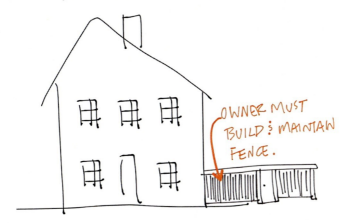

OWNER MUST BUILD & MAINTAIN FENCE.

COVENANTS

Affirmative covenants require action after the fact.

CONDITIONAL

CURRENT OWNER
DOESN'T PERFORM
REQUIREMENT
⬇
PROPERTY REVERTS
BACK TO PRIOR
[NO FENCE] OWNER

COVENANTS

Conditional covenants have contingent ownership.

LAND VALUES

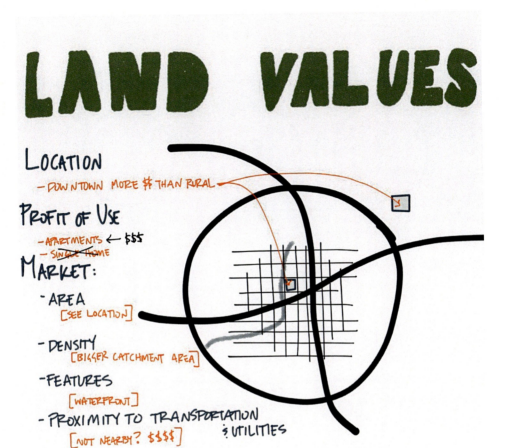

LOCATION
- DOWNTOWN MORE $$ THAN RURAL

PROFIT OF USE
- APARTMENTS ← $$$
- SINGLE HOME

MARKET:
- AREA
  [SEE LOCATION]

- DENSITY
  [BIGGER CATCHMENT AREA]

- FEATURES
  [WATERFRONT]

- PROXIMITY TO TRANSPORTATION
  [NOT NEARBY? $$$$] & UTILITIES

Land values affect every aspect of a project.

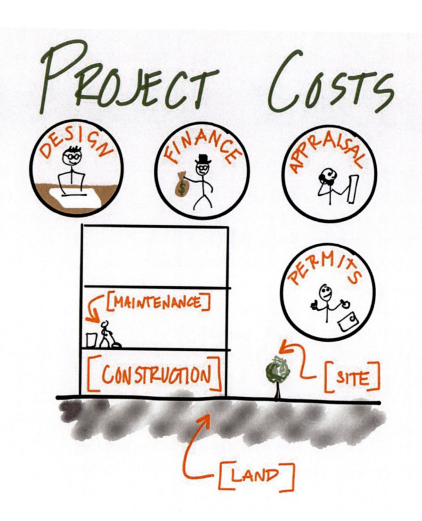

Project costs are seen and unseen.

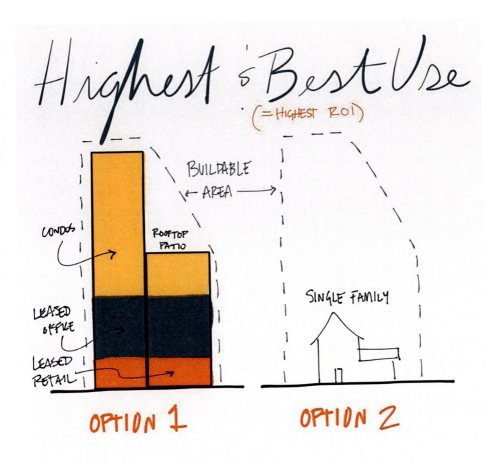

Highest & Best Use

(= HIGHEST ROI)

BUILDABLE
← AREA →

CONDOS

ROOFTOP PATIO

LEASED OFFICE

LEASED RETAIL

SINGLE FAMILY

OPTION 1

OPTION 2

The highest and best use of a space = most cost effective (from a zoning standpoint).

MARKET VALUATION

LAND/BUILDING PRICED TO REFLECT SIMILAR PROPERTY VALUES W/ ADJUSTMENTS FOR UNIQUENESS OF SITE

REALTORS CALL THIS "COMPS"

◻ SITE

▪ SIMILAR PROPERTIES FOR SALE OR RECENTLY SOLD

Market value is one of 3 ways to determine land/project costs.

UNIT PRICING

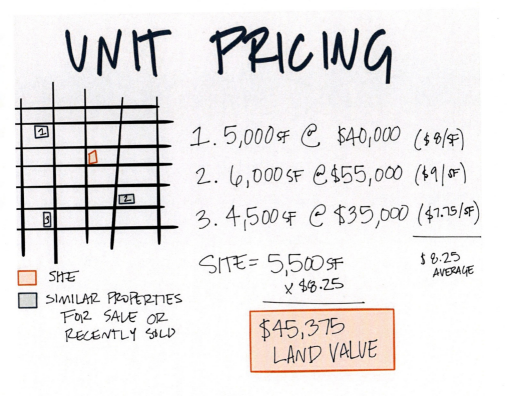

1. 5,000 SF @ $40,000 ($8/SF)

2. 6,000 SF @ $55,000 ($9/SF)

3. 4,500 SF @ $35,000 ($7.75/SF)

_____

$8.25
AVERAGE

SITE = 5,500 SF
x $8.25
_____

$45,375
LAND VALUE

□ SITE

□ SIMILAR PROPERTIES
FOR SALE OR
RECENTLY SOLD

Market value projections rely on unit pricing of nearby, similar properties.

COST VALUATION

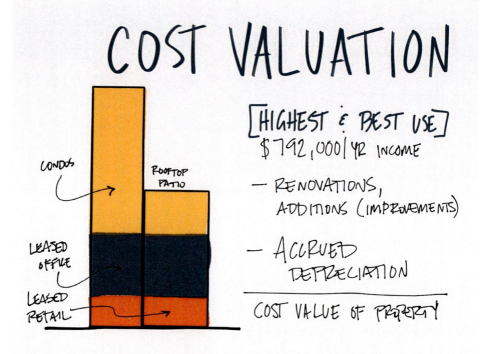

CONDOS

ROOFTOP PATIO

LEASED OFFICE

LEASED RETAIL

[HIGHEST & BEST USE]
$792,000/YR INCOME

— RENOVATIONS, ADDITIONS (IMPROVEMENTS)

— ACCRUED DEPRECIATION

COST VALUE OF PROPERTY

Cost valuation prices a project at the highest and best use.

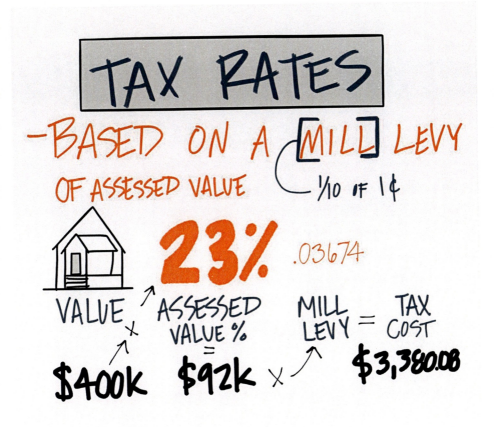

Understanding taxes is a major piece to the
financial health of the project.

Tax Incentive

TURNS UNECONOMICAL PROJECTS INTO VIABLE OPTIONS

TAX CREDITS FOR RENOVATING HISTORIC PROPERTIES

NEW BUSINESS ENCOURAGED BY REDUCED/ELIMINATED TAXES

Tax incentives can spur development or maintain quality.

Life Cycle Cost

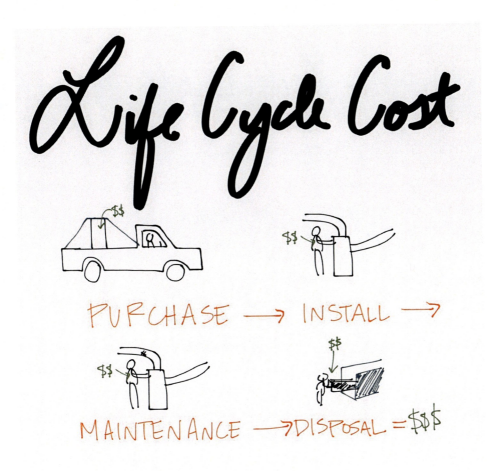

PURCHASE → INSTALL →

MAINTENANCE →DISPOSAL = $$$

Tracking costs through the life of a project: what the LCC is all about. This can be as broad as the entire building or as specific as a single piece of equipment.

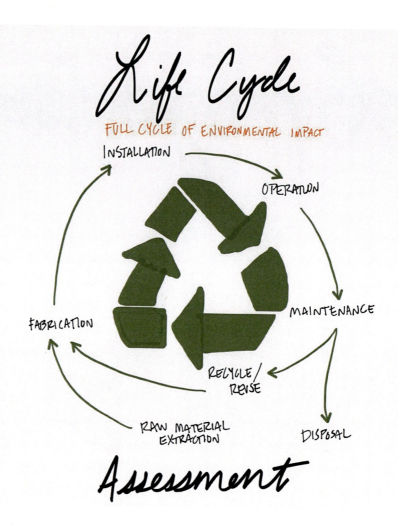

Life Cycle

FULL CYCLE OF ENVIRONMENTAL IMPACT

INSTALLATION

OPERATION

MAINTENANCE

FABRICATION

RECYCLE / REUSE

DISPOSAL

RAW MATERIAL EXTRACTION

Assessment

Life Cycle Assessments (LCAs) look at the environmental impact.

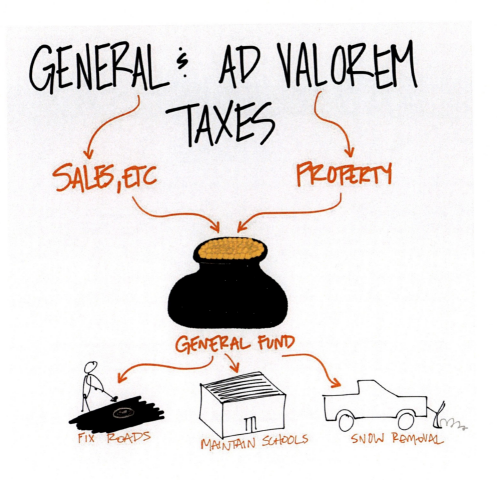

Let's talk taxes: general and property taxes are the two most basic forms.

Special TAX

FOR A SPECIFIC PURPOSE

RESTAURANT TAX

LUCAS OIL STADIUM

REQUIRES A MAJORITY VOTE OF PEOPLE IN THE DISTRICT

A special tax goes towards a specific public interest project.

GENERAL OBLIGATION BONDS

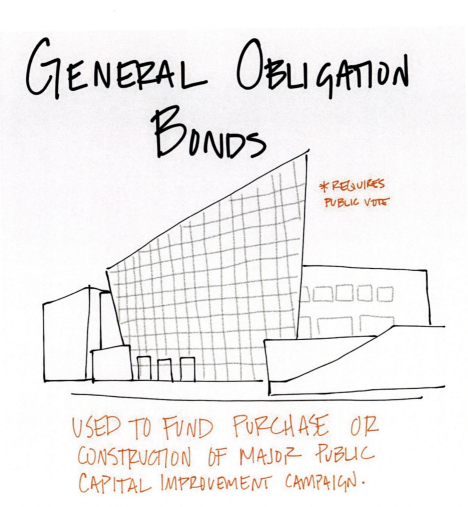

*REQUIRES PUBLIC VOTE

USED TO FUND PURCHASE OR CONSTRUCTION OF MAJOR PUBLIC CAPITAL IMPROVEMENT CAMPAIGN.

General obligation bonds fund public campaign improvements.

Revenue / Rate-Supported Bonds

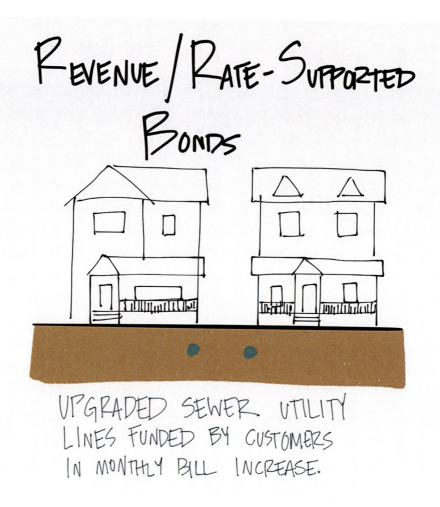

UPGRADED SEWER UTILITY
LINES FUNDED BY CUSTOMERS
IN MONTHLY BILL INCREASE.

Rate bonds help fund utility improvements.

PUBLIC ENTERPRISE

BOND TO FUND CONSTRUCTION IS PAID OFF WITH FACILITIES REVENUES.

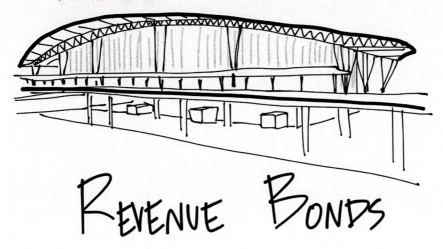

REVENUE BONDS

Public enterprise revenue bonds are paid off with fees from the facility they fund.

Development

CAN BE CONTROVERSIAL

DEVELOPER PAYS FEES TO MAINTAIN/
IMPROVE UTILITIES AND STREET IMPROVEMENTS

Impact Fees

Development impact fees are paid by the developer to improve utilities.

Subdivision exactions fund public spaces (or they should).

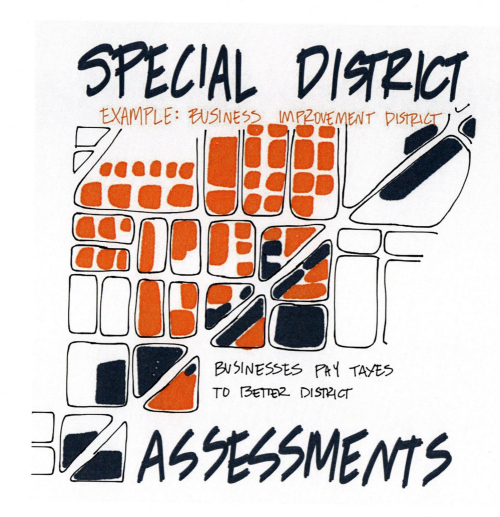

SPECIAL DISTRICT

EXAMPLE: BUSINESS IMPROVEMENT DISTRICT

BUSINESSES PAY TAXES
TO BETTER DISTRICT

ASSESSMENTS

Special district assessments tax businesses for public cultural improvements.

Blanket

Loans

DEVELOPER GETS LOAN FOR ENTIRE PROPERTY. AS LOTS SELL, CHUNKS OF LOAN ARE PAID BACK.

Blanket loans cover the purchase of large masses of land for development of individual parcels.

Bonds

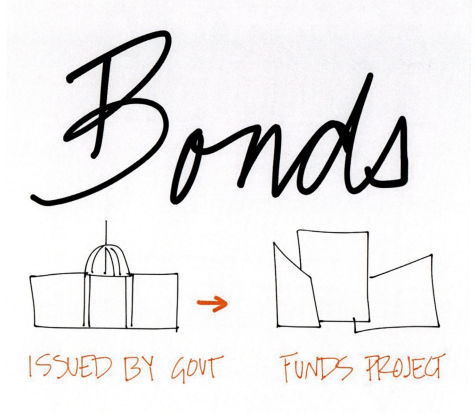

ISSUED BY GOVT → FUNDS PROJECT

Bonds are issued by the government to fund projects.

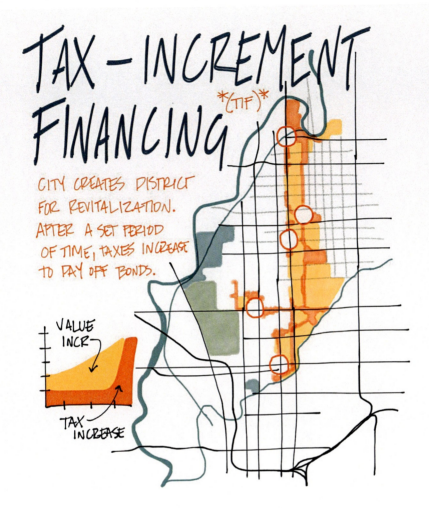

TAX – INCREMENT FINANCING *(TIF)*

CITY CREATES DISTRICT FOR REVITALIZATION. AFTER A SET PERIOD OF TIME, TAXES INCREASE TO PAY OFF BONDS.

VALUE INCR

TAX INCREASE

TIFs create districts to fund public improvement.

BRIDGE

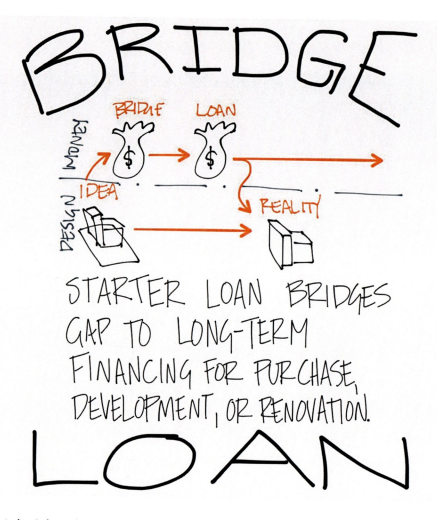

STARTER LOAN BRIDGES GAP TO LONG-TERM FINANCING FOR PURCHASE, DEVELOPMENT, OR RENOVATION.

LOAN

A bridge loan does just that - it bridges the paperwork delay of getting a project started.

Construction

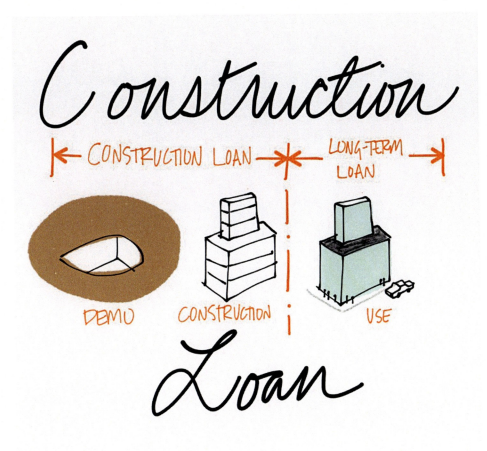

|← CONSTRUCTION LOAN →|← LONG-TERM LOAN →|

DEMO CONSTRUCTION USE

Loan

Construction loans transition to long-term loans upon project completion.

HARD MONEY LOAN

— LOAN WITH HIGH INTEREST, TYPICALLY FOR FAST TURNOVER (FLIP) OR DIRE SITUATION.

FLIP
(ALLOWS QUICK FUNDS)

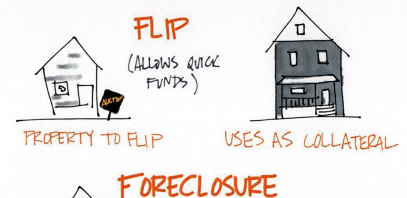

PROPERTY TO FLIP   USES AS COLLATERAL

FORECLOSURE

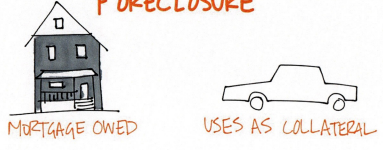

MORTGAGE OWED   USES AS COLLATERAL

Hard money loans are a worst case scenario.

Mezzanine Loan

COLLATERAL FOR LOAN IS MADE OF STOCK IN DEVELOPER'S COMPANY.

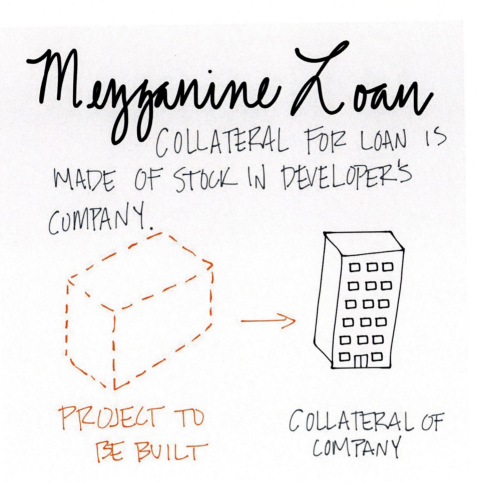

PROJECT TO BE BUILT

COLLATERAL OF COMPANY

A mezzanine loan holds collateral in the company, not the building.

Pro Forma

[AS A MATTER OF FORM]

-TEST MODEL/STATEMENT THAT
HELPS DETERMINE FINANCIAL
FEASIBILITY.

— LANDCOST
—DESIGN FEES
— CONSTRUCTION

— MAINTENANCE

+ RENTAL OR
SALE INCOME

NEEDS TO BE + AFTER
A CERTAIN PERIOD OF TIME

Statement

A pro forma shows the financial viability of a project.

MORTGAGE LOAN

BANK PROVIDES MONEY TO PURCHASE PROPERTY IN EXCHANGE FOR LIEN UNTIL DEBT IS PAID.

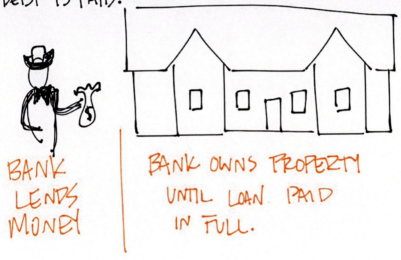

BANK LENDS MONEY

BANK OWNS PROPERTY UNTIL LOAN PAID IN FULL.

A mortgage loan is the loan type we are probably all the most familiar with: money from bank + bank owns house until mortgage is paid.

SURVEYS PT 1:

SITE FEATURES

There are a couple parts to surveys; the first is site features. Everyone loves a pretty view.

SURVEYS Pt2:

AS-BUILTS

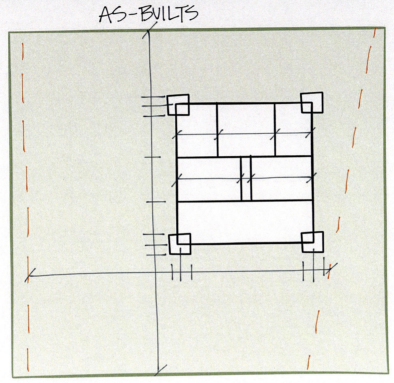

Another key to a good survey are the as-builts.

SURVEYS PT3:
STRUCTURE

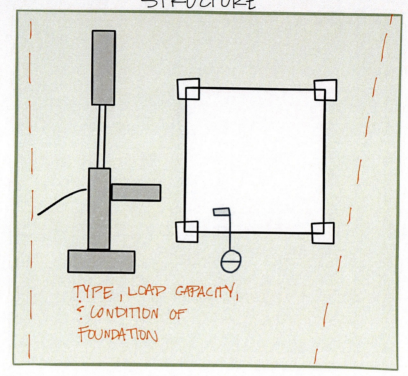

TYPE, LOAD CAPACITY,
& CONDITION OF
FOUNDATION

The as-builts will show structure, but it's important to survey existing conditions.

SURVEYS PT4:

ROOF

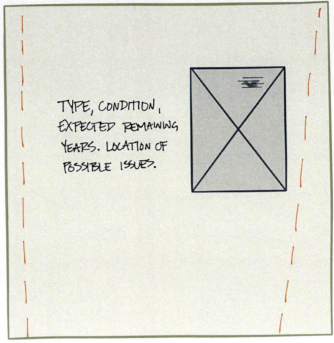

TYPE, CONDITION, EXPECTED REMAINING YEARS. LOCATION OF POSSIBLE ISSUES.

Roofs are boring, but they keep the elements out. Survey what's in place to know that you won't have an indoor swimming pool in the future.

SURVEYS PT5:
EXTERIOR ENVELOPE

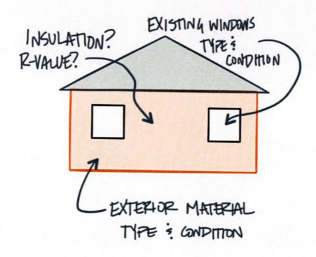

INSULATION?
R-VALUE?

EXISTING WINDOWS
TYPE &
CONDITION

EXTERIOR MATERIAL
TYPE & CONDITION

Elevations, especially of significant features, are important to note.

SURVEYS PT6:

MECHANICAL SYSTEM

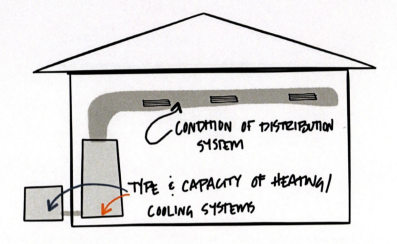

CONDITION OF DISTRIBUTION SYSTEM

TYPE & CAPACITY OF HEATING/ COOLING SYSTEMS

MEP...it will make or break your design details.

SURVEYS PT 7:

PLUMBING SYSTEM

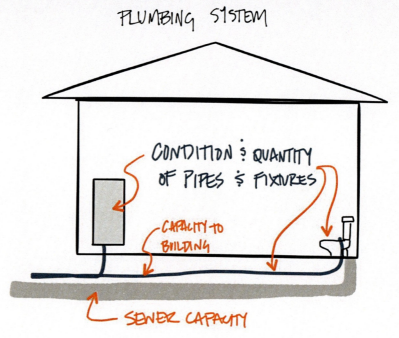

CONDITION & QUANTITY OF PIPES & FIXTURES

CAPACITY TO BUILDING

SEWER CAPACITY

As we've seen in Flint, old pipes can wreak havoc. It's important to survey existing plumbing as a part of any renovation/addition.

SURVEYS PT 8:
ELECTRICAL

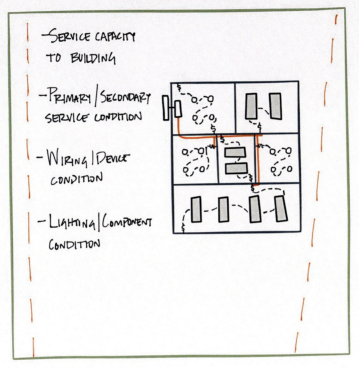

- Service Capacity to Building

- Primary / Secondary Service Condition

- Wiring / Device Condition

- Lighting / Component Condition

From experience: knob & tube is a nightmare and people like to add to circuits willy-nilly. Check your electrical systems when you survey.

SURVEYS Pt 9:
FIRE

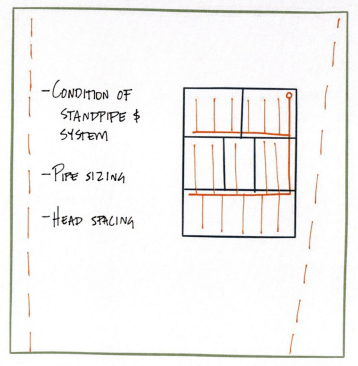

- Condition of standpipe & system
- Pipe sizing
- Head spacing

Most surveys show a need for updated/added sprinkler systems. Keep them in mind because this is not a cheap prospect.

SURVEYS PT 10:

EQUIPMENT & FINISHES

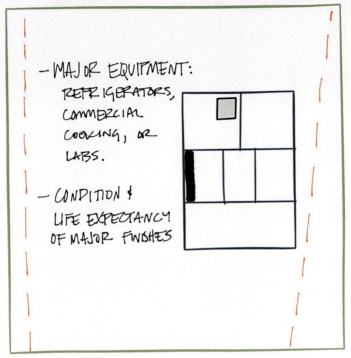

- MAJOR EQUIPMENT:
  REFRIGERATORS,
  COMMERCIAL
  COOKING, OR
  LABS.

- CONDITION &
  LIFE EXPECTANCY
  OF MAJOR FINISHES

Major equipment should be checked for condition and life expectancy. Their cost of replacement quickly adds to project costs.

SURVEYS PT II:

COST & TIME CONSTRAINTS

[NOT TECHNICALLY PART OF SURVEY]

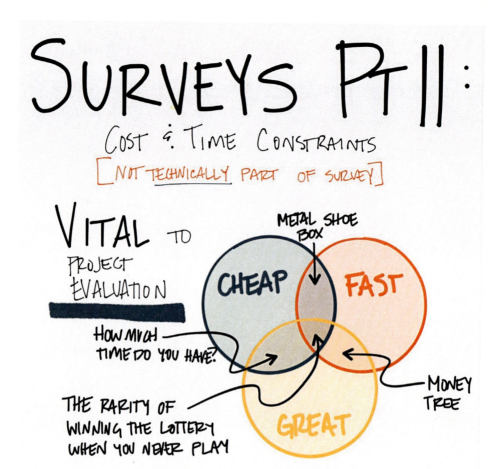

VITAL TO PROJECT EVALUATION

METAL SHOE BOX

CHEAP   FAST

HOW MUCH TIME DO YOU HAVE?

MONEY TREE

THE RARITY OF WINNING THE LOTTERY WHEN YOU NEVER PLAY

GREAT

Know your cost and time constraints. No one likes a metal box and there's always a compromise to decide on.

SURVEYS PT|2:

DOCUMENTATION

- MANUAL DRAWINGS
  > 1/4" - 1/2" ACCURACY
- CAD

- NOTES

- REPORTS

- PHOTOGRAPHS/VIDEOS

> IF THERE ARE ANY EXISTING DOCUMENTS, THEY SHOULD BE COLLECTED.

Surveys all boil down to one thing: document the crap out of that building.

SURVEYS Pt|3:

REGULATION WRAP-UP

- ☑ ZONING & EASEMENT RESTRICTIONS
- ☑ DEED & COVENANT RESTRICTIONS
- ☑ HISTORIC PRESERVATION RULES
- ☑ LOCAL & ENERGY CODES
- ☑ DETERMINE CONSTRUCTION TYPE & OCCUPANCY

There are a variety of regulations required/ helpful to a survey.

MEASURING/RECORDING METHODS:

HAND MEASURING ÷ DRAFTING

PRO	CON
- GOOD FOR SMALL DETAILS	- HIGH POTENTIAL FOR ERRORS
- LESS SKILL / SPECIFIC TRAINING	- LABOR INTENSIVE

Hand-measuring is cheap, but prone to errors.

MEASURING/RECORDING METHODS:

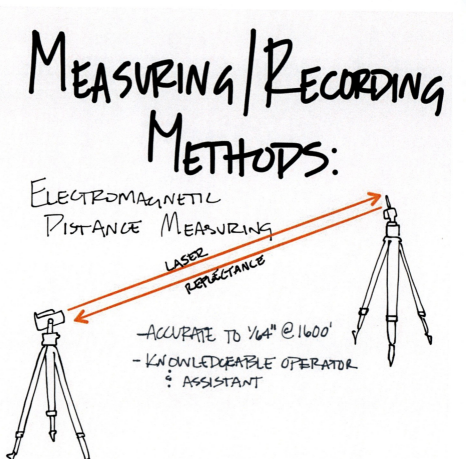

ELECTROMAGNETIC
DISTANCE MEASURING

LASER
REFLECTANCE

- ACCURATE TO ¼" @ 1600'
- KNOWLEDGEABLE OPERATOR
  & ASSISTANT

Electromagnetic measurement requires 2 field technicians and a reflector.

Measuring/Recording Methods:

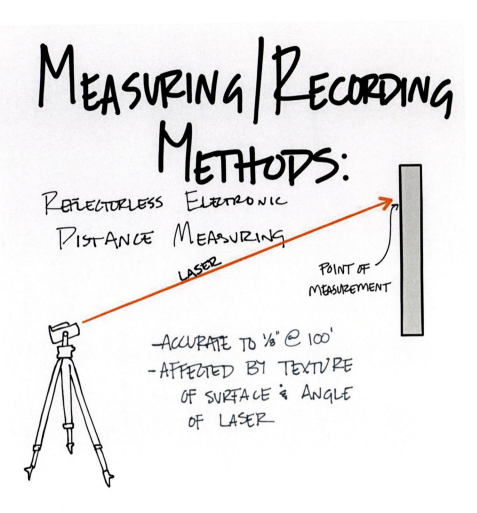

Reflectorless Electronic
Distance Measuring

LASER

POINT OF
MEASUREMENT

- ACCURATE TO ⅛" @ 100'
- AFFECTED BY TEXTURE
  OF SURFACE & ANGLE
  OF LASER

The accuracy of a reflectorless EDM is impacted by angle or texture of reflecting material.

MEASURING/RECORDING METHODS:

RECTIFIED PHOTOGRAPHY

- FILM-BASED, LARGE FORMAT
- NO DISTORTION

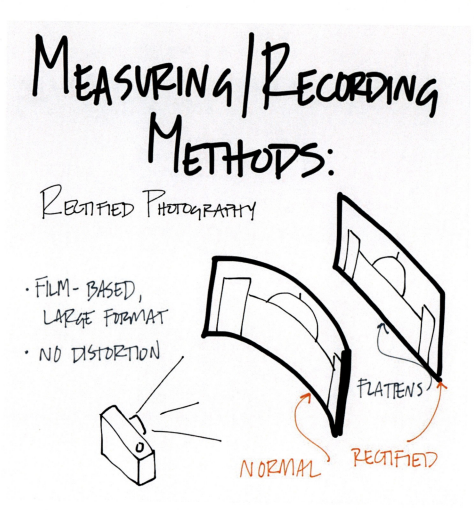

NORMAL   RECTIFIED   FLATTENS

Rectified photography uses large format film to remove distortion.

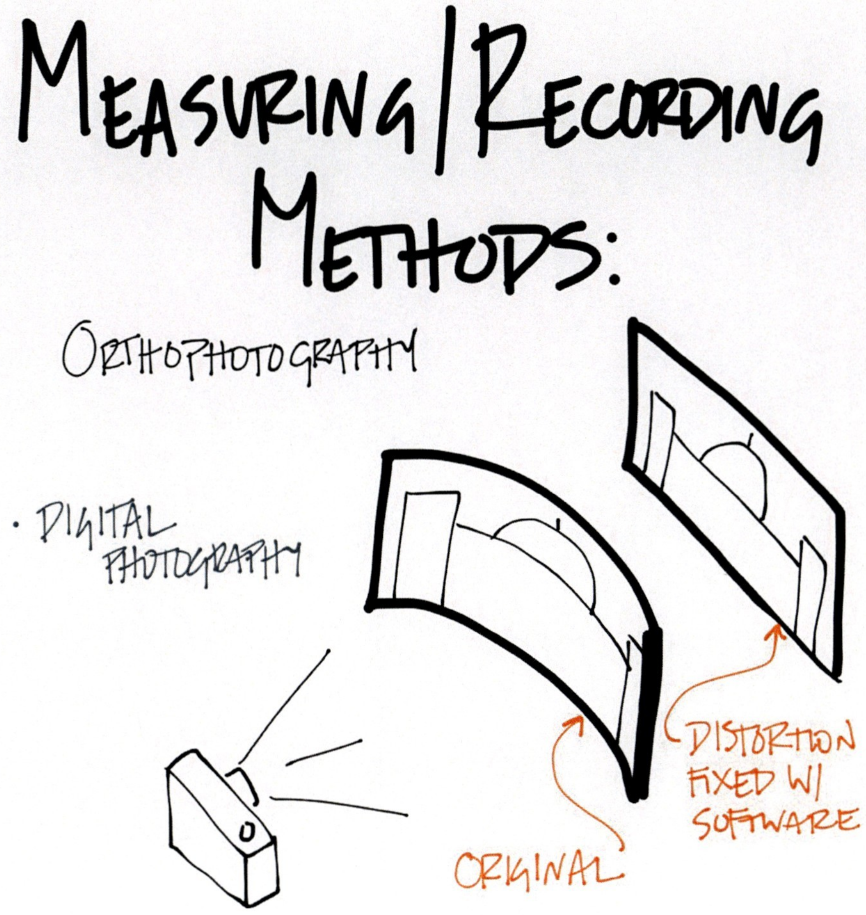

MEASURING/RECORDING METHODS:

ORTHOPHOTOGRAPHY

· DIGITAL PHOTOGRAPHY

ORIGINAL

DISTORTION FIXED W/ SOFTWARE

Orthophotography fixes image distortion after the fact.

Measuring/Recording Methods:
Photogrammetry

Stereophotogrammetry

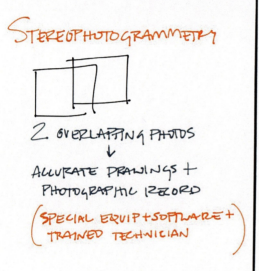

2 overlapping photos
↓
accurate drawings + photographic record

(special equip + software + trained technician)

Convergent Photogrammetry

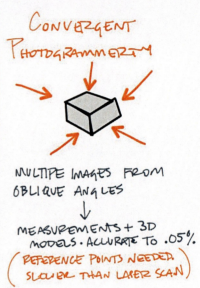

Multiple images from oblique angles
↓
measurements + 3D models. Accurate to .05%.

(reference points needed. slower than laser scan)

There are two types of photogrammetry: stereo and convergent.

Measuring/Recording Methods:

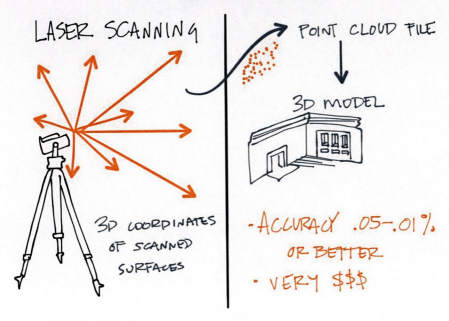

LASER SCANNING

3D COORDINATES OF SCANNED SURFACES

POINT CLOUD FILE

3D MODEL

- ACCURACY .05–.01% OR BETTER
- VERY $$$

Laser scanning creates a point cloud.

Evaluating Existing Structures

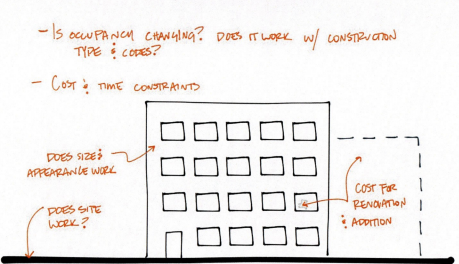

- Is occupancy changing? Does it work w/ construction type & codes?

- Cost & time constraints

DOES SIZE & APPEARANCE WORK

DOES SITE WORK?

COST FOR RENOVATION & ADDITION

The evaluation of existing structures requires a keen eye.

RENOVATING HISTORIC STRUCTURES

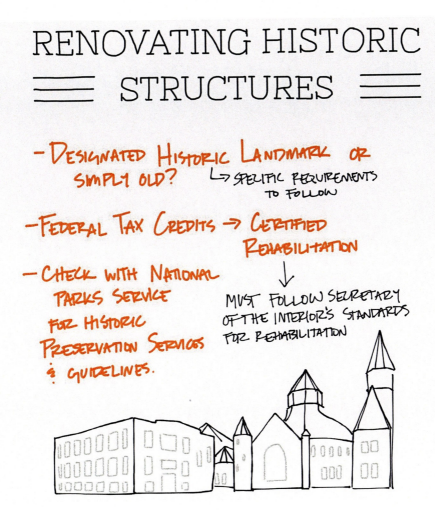

- DESIGNATED HISTORIC LANDMARK OR SIMPLY OLD? ⤷ SPECIFIC REQUIREMENTS TO FOLLOW

- FEDERAL TAX CREDITS → CERTIFIED REHABILITATION ↓

- CHECK WITH NATIONAL PARKS SERVICE FOR HISTORIC PRESERVATION SERVICES & GUIDELINES.

MUST FOLLOW SECRETARY OF THE INTERIOR'S STANDARDS FOR REHABILITATION

When renovating historic structures, a plan must be in place.

HISTORIC PROJECT

PRESERVATION	REHABILITATION	RESTORATION	RECONSTRUCTION
- RETAIN ALL HISTORIC FABRIC	- KEEPS & MAINTAINS MATERIALS	- SNAPSHOT IN TIME, FOCUSES ON ONE SPECIFIC ARCHITECTURAL PERIOD	- LEAST HISTORICALLY ACCURATE
- CONSERVATION, MAINTENANCE, & REPAIR	- CAN REPLACE W/ MORE MODERN MATERIALS BECAUSE IT ASSUMES BLDG NEEDS MASSIVE REPAIR	- REMOVES MATERIAL & CHARACTER FROM OTHER TIME PERIODS	- RECREATE A NON-SURVIVING SITE, LANDSCAPE, BUILDING, ETC
	- FOCUS ON OVERALL CHARACTER		

* DESIGNATED LANDMARKS SHOULD CONTACT STATE HISTORIC PRESERVATION OFFICER (CALLED "SHPO")

Historic projects fall into four main categories.

SECRETARY OF THE INTERIOR'S STANDARDS FOR REHABILITATION

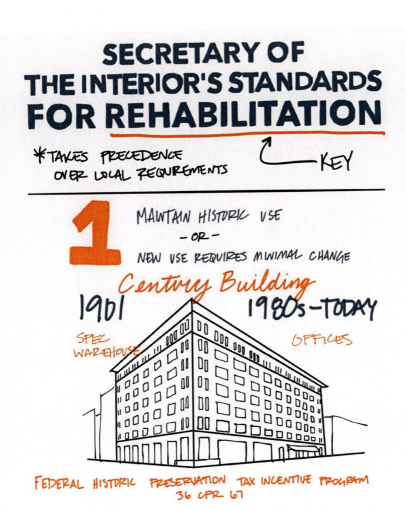

*TAKES PRECEDENCE OVER LOCAL REQUIREMENTS

↰— KEY

1 MAINTAIN HISTORIC USE
— OR —
NEW USE REQUIRES MINIMAL CHANGE

Century Building

1901   1980s–TODAY

SPEC WAREHOUSE   OFFICES

FEDERAL HISTORIC PRESERVATION TAX INCENTIVE PROGRAM
36 CFR 67

A look at the Secretary of the Interior's Standards for Rehabilitation. Rule 1: Thou shalt maintain or make minimal change.

SECRETARY OF THE INTERIOR'S STANDARDS FOR REHABILITATION

*TAKES PRECEDENCE OVER LOCAL REQUIREMENTS  KEY

2 PRESERVE HISTORIC CHARACTER:
DO NOT REMOVE OR ALTER DISTINCTIVE FEATURES, SPACES, OR SPATIAL RELATIONSHIPS.

FEDERAL HISTORIC PRESERVATION TAX INCENTIVE PROGRAM
36 CFR 67

Rule 2: The historic face stays in place.

SECRETARY OF THE INTERIOR'S STANDARDS FOR REHABILITATION

*TAKES PRECEDENCE OVER LOCAL REQUIREMENTS

↑ KEY

3 PHYSICAL RECORD OF TIME, PLACE, & USE

CHANGES NOT TRUE IN HISTORICAL NATURE ARE NOT ALLOWED.

NOT OF CORRECT ERA

FEDERAL HISTORIC PRESERVATION TAX INCENTIVE PROGRAM 36 CFR 67

Rule 3: Thou shalt not mix eras, decades, and styles.

SECRETARY OF THE INTERIOR'S STANDARDS FOR REHABILITATION

*TAKES PRECEDENCE OVER LOCAL REQUIREMENTS ——KEY

4 PREVIOUS CHANGES WITH THEIR OWN HISTORIC SIGNIFICANCE WILL BE KEPT.

NEWER AWNING NOW A PART OF HISTORIC FABRIC.

FEDERAL HISTORIC PRESERVATION TAX INCENTIVE PROGRAM
36 CFR 67

Rule 4: Keep the less-old important stuff.

SECRETARY OF THE INTERIOR'S STANDARDS FOR REHABILITATION

*TAKES PRECEDENCE OVER LOCAL REQUIREMENTS

↳ KEY

5 DISTINCTIVE FEATURES, FINISHES, OR CONSTRUCTION TECHNIQUES SHOULD BE KEPT.

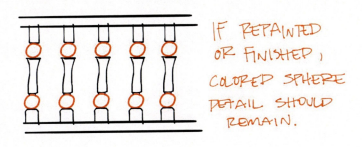

IF REPAINTED OR FINISHED, COLORED SPHERE DETAIL SHOULD REMAIN.

FEDERAL HISTORIC PRESERVATION TAX INCENTIVE PROGRAM
36 CFR 67

Rule 5: Keep the techniques that are distinct.

SECRETARY OF THE INTERIOR'S STANDARDS FOR REHABILITATION

*TAKES PRECEDENCE OVER LOCAL REQUIREMENTS

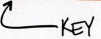 KEY

6 REPAIR BEFORE REPLACE

IF DETERIORATION IS SEVERE, REPLACEMENT SHOULD MATCH COLOR, TEXTURE, & MATERIALS.

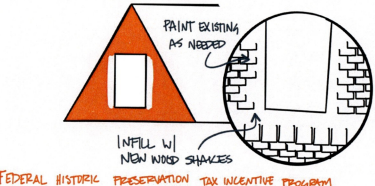

PAINT EXISTING AS NEEDED

INFILL W/ NEW WOOD SHAKES

FEDERAL HISTORIC PRESERVATION TAX INCENTIVE PROGRAM
36 CFR 67

Rule 6: Repair trumps replace. Keep the old as long as you can.

SECRETARY OF THE INTERIOR'S STANDARDS FOR REHABILITATION

*TAKES PRECEDENCE OVER LOCAL REQUIREMENTS

⌐—KEY

7 BE GENTLE
CHEMICAL OR PHYSICAL TREATMENT WILL USE THE GENTLEST MEANS POSSIBLE.

POWER WASH

SOFT CLOTH ✓

FEDERAL HISTORIC PRESERVATION TAX INCENTIVE PROGRAM
36 CFR 67

Rule 7: Don't damage the material trying to clean it.

SECRETARY OF
THE INTERIOR'S STANDARDS
FOR REHABILITATION

*TAKES PRECEDENCE
OVER LOCAL REQUIREMENTS

KEY

8 PRESERVE ARCHAEOLOGY

IF FOUND, PROPER AUTHORITIES MUST
BE CONTACTED TO MITIGATE DAMAGE.

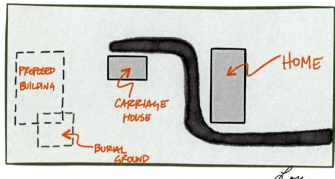

FEDERAL HISTORIC PRESERVATION TAX INCENTIVE PROGRAM
36 CFR 67

Rule 8: No Indiana Jones allowed. The loot should
be preserved.

SECRETARY OF THE INTERIOR'S STANDARDS FOR REHABILITATION

*TAKES PRECEDENCE OVER LOCAL REQUIREMENTS KEY

9 NEW ≠ TRUMP OLD
NEW ADDITIONS/ALTERATIONS SHOULD NOT DESTROY MATERIALS OR SPATIAL RELATIONSHIPS.

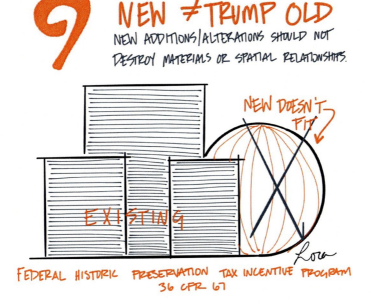

NEW DOESN'T FIT

EXISTING

FEDERAL HISTORIC PRESERVATION TAX INCENTIVE PROGRAM
36 CFR 67

Rule 9: New never takes precedent in rehabilitation.

SECRETARY OF THE INTERIOR'S STANDARDS FOR REHABILITATION

*TAKES PRECEDENCE OVER LOCAL REQUIREMENTS

KEY

10 DO NO HARM

ADDITIONS SHOULD NOT IMPACT HISTORIC STRUCTURE IN A WAY THAT IT'S REMOVAL DOES NOT AFFECT THE BUILDING.

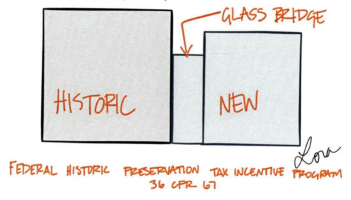

GLASS BRIDGE

HISTORIC

NEW

FEDERAL HISTORIC PRESERVATION TAX INCENTIVE PROGRAM
36 CFR 67

Rule 10: First do no harm. (This is the overall mantra of architecture, too.)

1 HISTORIC USE OR REFLECTION OF RESTORATION PERIOD.

2 SIGNIFICANT MATERIAL & FEATURES PRESERVED.

3 PHYSICAL RECORD OF TIME

4 FEATURES OF OTHER PERIODS DOCUMENTED & REMOVED.

5 MATERIALS, FINISHES, ETC OF RESTORATION ERA KEPT.

6 REPAIR > REPLACE

7 REPLACEMENT OF MISSING FEATURES MUST BE SUBSTANTIATED W/ DOCS

8 GENTLE TREATMENTS

9 PRESERVE ARCHAEOLOGY

10 UNEXECUTED DESIGNS WILL NOT BE UNDERTAKEN

Lora

U.S. NATIONAL PARK SERVICE
STANDARDS FOR RESTORATION

The National Parks Service standards are slightly different than rehabilitation standards.

SURVEYING HISTORIC STRUCTURES

NORMAL SURVEY

+

SETTLEMENT, DEFLECTION, OR DAMAGED STRUCTURAL MEMBERS	DETERMINE HISTORIC ELEMENTS REMOVED OR ALTERED	PRIORITIZE HISTORIC CHARACTER: - FORM - MATERIAL - SPACE - WORKMANSHIP - ETC

Historical structures require more than a normal survey.

NATIONAL PARK SERVICE RECOMMENDATIONS FOR MASONRY

identify, retain, and preserve

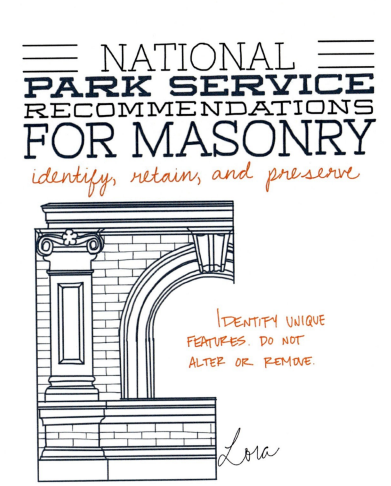

IDENTIFY UNIQUE FEATURES. DO NOT ALTER OR REMOVE.

Lora

The guidelines for masonry are similar: identify and preserve.

NATIONAL PARK SERVICE RECOMMENDATIONS FOR MASONRY

protect and maintain

PROTECT:
DRAIN &
    MAINTAIN

CLEAN:
GENTLY.
NO SANDBLASTING.

PAINT:
REMOVE IF DAMAGED.
RESTORE VIA HISTORIC
DOCUMENTATION.

Protect, clean, and maintain. Simple steps to keep masonry healthy.

NATIONAL PARK SERVICE RECOMMENDATIONS FOR MASONRY

repair

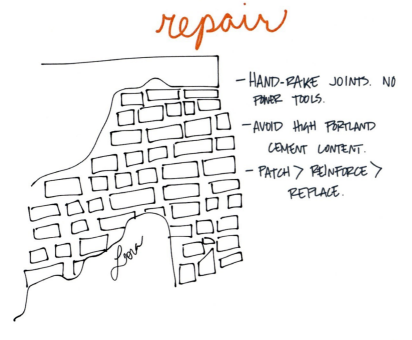

- HAND-RAKE JOINTS. NO POWER TOOLS.
- AVOID HIGH PORTLAND CEMENT CONTENT.
- PATCH > REINFORCE > REPLACE.

Any masonry repairs should be made by hand, gently.

NATIONAL PARK SERVICE RECOMMENDATIONS FOR MASONRY

replace

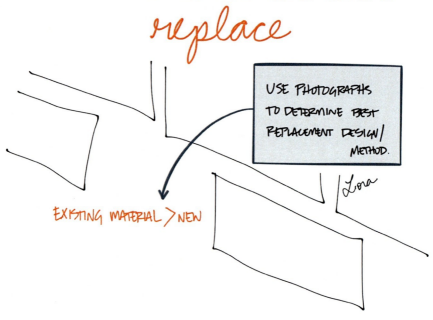

USE PHOTOGRAPHS TO DETERMINE BEST REPLACEMENT DESIGN/ METHOD.

Lora

EXISTING MATERIAL > NEW

If you do replace masonry, use similar age/ material/color.

NATIONAL
PARK SERVICE
RECOMMENDATIONS
FOR MASONRY

remove existing features from other historic periods

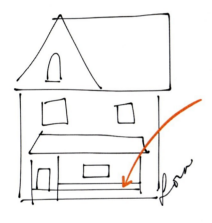

REMOVE BRICK FEATURES OF FRONT PORCH & RESTORE TO QUEEN ANNE-ERA POSTS. SAVE BRICK FEATURES (IF SIGNIFICANT) TO STUDY.

Remove masonry used in a post-restoration era style.

NATIONAL
PARK SERVICE
RECOMMENDATIONS
FOR MASONRY

recreate missing features

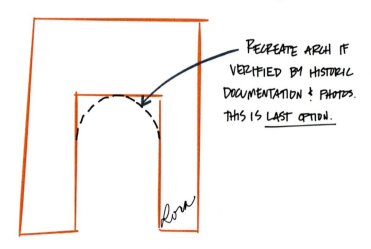

RECREATE ARCH IF VERIFIED BY HISTORIC DOCUMENTATION & PHOTOS. THIS IS LAST OPTION.

Restoration is our best educated guess at recreation.

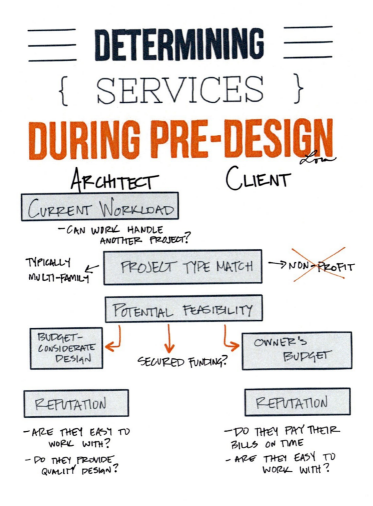

DETERMINING

{ SERVICES }

DURING PRE-DESIGN

ARCHITECT — **CLIENT**

CURRENT WORKLOAD
—CAN WORK HANDLE ANOTHER PROJECT?

TYPICALLY MULTI-FAMILY ← **PROJECT TYPE MATCH** → NON-PROFIT

POTENTIAL FEASIBILITY

BUDGET-CONSIDERATE DESIGN ← SECURED FUNDING? → **OWNER'S BUDGET**

REPUTATION
—ARE THEY EASY TO WORK WITH?
—DO THEY PROVIDE QUALITY DESIGN?

REPUTATION
—DO THEY PAY THEIR BILLS ON TIME
—ARE THEY EASY TO WORK WITH?

Playing matchmaker with a client involves a lot of variables.

DETERMINING { SERVICES } DURING PRE-DESIGN

JOB ACCEPTED

- DETERMINE SCOPE
- DETERMINE FEE
- DETERMINE SCHEDUE

When you accept a job or a client accepts you, it's time for a plan.

DETERMINING
{ SERVICES }
DURING PRE-DESIGN

WORK > BUDGET

- DECLINE JOB

- NEGOTIATE SCOPE / BUDGET

- ACCEPT LOWER PROFIT

  ↳ LAST RESORT

Money is almost always an issue, so know the budget as soon as possible.

DETERMINING

{ SERVICES }

DURING PRE-DESIGN

NEW ARCHITECT

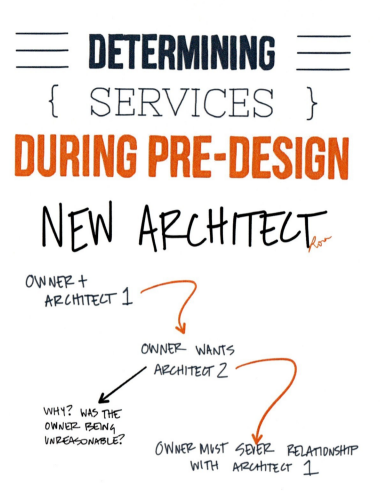

OWNER +
ARCHITECT 1

OWNER WANTS
ARCHITECT 2

WHY? WAS THE
OWNER BEING
UNREASONABLE?

OWNER MUST SEVER RELATIONSHIP
WITH ARCHITECT 1

If you're the replacement architect, get your ducks in a row and find out why.

COORDINATION WITH A REGULATORY AGENCY

ARCHITECT WILL:

- CREATE PRELIM SITE PLANS & PROPOSALS, & PRELIMINARY BUILDING DESIGNS

- MEET WITH GOVERNMENT AGENCIES OR LOCAL NEIGHBORHOOD GROUPS

THIS IS NOT A PART OF THE BUILDING DESIGN FEE. THIS IS AN ADDITIONAL FEE.
Love

Coordination with agencies or code consultants isn't in the basic design budget.

COORDINATION WITH A REGULATORY AGENCY

Lora

UNIQUE DESIGN MAY PRESENT CHALLENGES

↓

VARIANCE

↓

ARCHITECT WILL WORK WITH OFFICIALS & CONSULTANTS FOR APPROVAL OF VARIANCES

When a project is irregular, the architect helps the client coordinate with officials and consultants.

CONSULTANTS

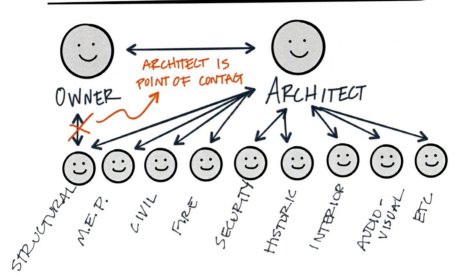

In most instances, the architect is the point of contact for the owner.

Contracts

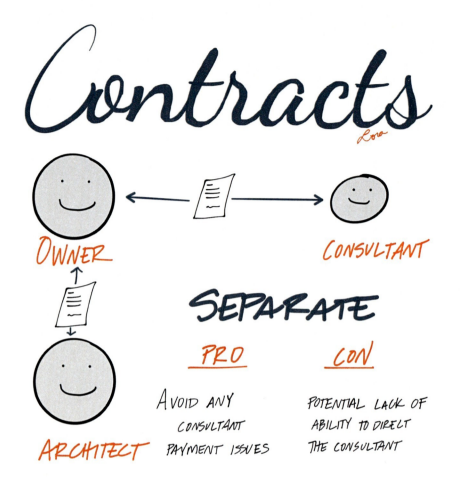

OWNER

CONSULTANT

SEPARATE

PRO

CON

AVOID ANY CONSULTANT PAYMENT ISSUES

POTENTIAL LACK OF ABILITY TO DIRECT THE CONSULTANT

ARCHITECT

There are pros and cons to maintaining a contract separate from the consultant.

Contracts

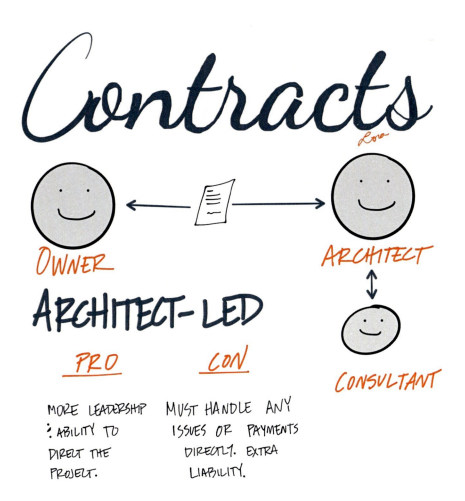

OWNER

ARCHITECT

CONSULTANT

ARCHITECT-LED

PRO

MORE LEADERSHIP & ABILITY TO DIRECT THE PROJECT.

CON

MUST HANDLE ANY ISSUES OR PAYMENTS DIRECTLY. EXTRA LIABILITY.

Architect-led contracts give you more leadership and liability.

CODES

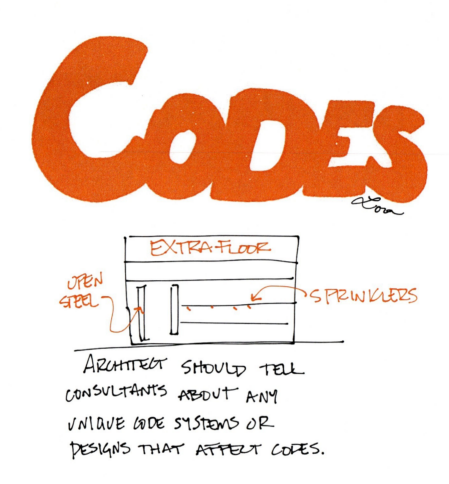

EXTRA·FLOOR

OPEN STEEL

SPRINKLERS

ARCHITECT SHOULD TELL CONSULTANTS ABOUT ANY UNIQUE CODE SYSTEMS OR DESIGNS THAT AFFECT CODES.

Open steel? Sprinklers washing the atrium glass? Be on the same page.

CODES

AIA C401

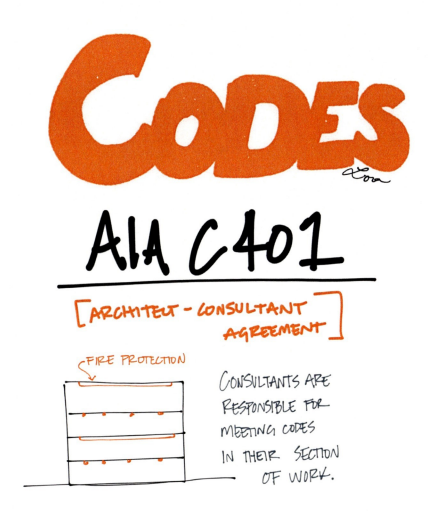

FIRE PROTECTION

CONSULTANTS ARE RESPONSIBLE FOR MEETING CODES IN THEIR SECTION OF WORK.

Contracts help make sure responsible parties stay accountable.

CODES

AIA B101

ARCHITECT IS
RESPONSIBLE TO
OWNER FOR
CODE COMPLIANCE.

AIA B101 solidifies your (legal) relationship with the owner.

210

PROGRAMMING

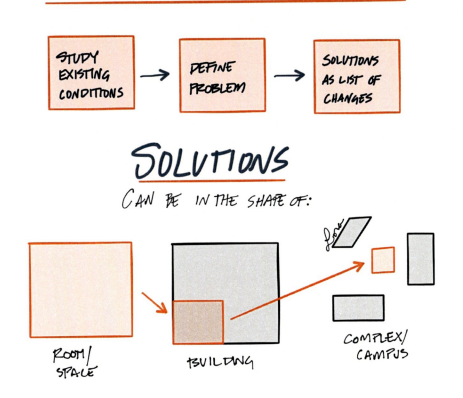

STUDY EXISTING CONDITIONS → DEFINE PROBLEM → SOLUTIONS AS LIST OF CHANGES

SOLUTIONS

CAN BE IN THE SHAPE OF:

ROOM/SPACE

BUILDING

COMPLEX/CAMPUS

Programming studies, defines, and solves a problem.

PROGRAMMING

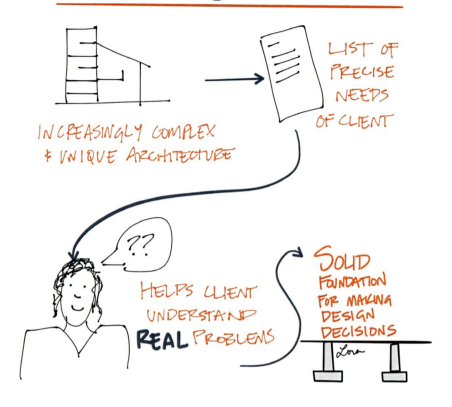

Good programming provides a foundation for making design decisions.

PROGRAMMING

CLIENT

- GOALS & OBJECTIVES

PROJECT

- SITE ANALYTICS
- AESTHETICS
- SPACE NEEDS
    - ADJACENCY REQUIREMENTS
    - ORGANIZING CONCEPTS
    - OUTDOOR SPACE NEEDS
- CODES
- BUDGETING
- SCHEDULE LIMITATIONS

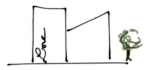

Programming starts to outline the space planning needs a project.

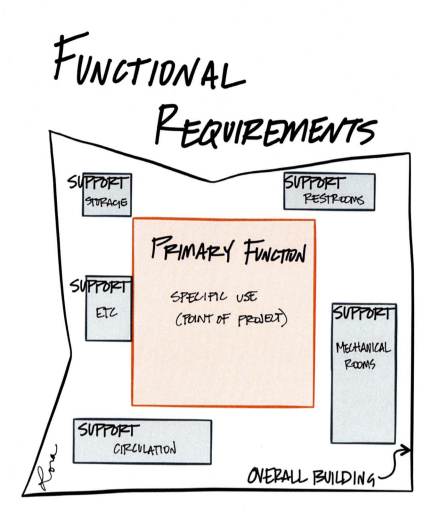

Programming creates a list of functional requirements within the overall building.

SPACE / VOLUME

CLIENT PROVIDES:

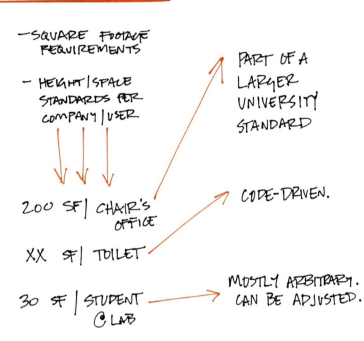

- SQUARE FOOTAGE REQUIREMENTS

- HEIGHT / SPACE STANDARDS PER COMPANY / USER

200 SF | CHAIR'S OFFICE

XX SF | TOILET

30 SF | STUDENT @ LAB

PART OF A LARGER UNIVERSITY STANDARD

CODE-DRIVEN.

MOSTLY ARBITRARY. CAN BE ADJUSTED.

In determining the spaces needed for a project, the architect narrows the wishlist.

SPACE / VOLUME

If AREAS NOT DEFINED BY CLIENT:

PER PERSON:

5-7 SF/PERSON
STANDING   X   X PEOPLE

PER EQUIPMENT:

AHU

CLEARANCE
FOR AIR
HANDLING UNIT

PER USE:

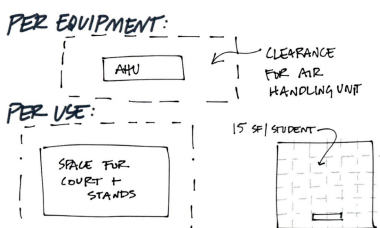

SPACE FOR
COURT +
STANDS

15 SF/STUDENT

Space sizing can be per person, use, or equipment.

SPACE PLANNING

✳ SQUARE FOOT ALLOTMENTS COVER PERSON, TASK, CIRCULATION, AND ANY ACCESSORY EQUIPMENT

100-250 SQ FEET

OFFICE

15-20 SF/ STUDENT

CLASSROOM

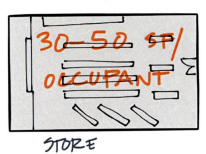

30-50 SF/ OCCUPANT

STORE

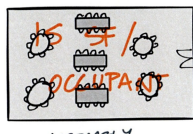

15 SF/ OCCUPANT

ASSEMBLY
(W/ MOVABLE SEATS)

Square footage allotments can be for person or use.

SPACE PLANNING

One

SOMETIMES THE SPACE PLANNING
DATA DICTATES ANOTHER AREA'S SIZE

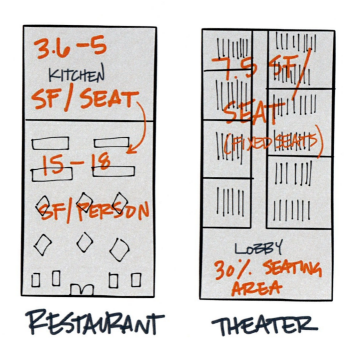

RESTAURANT   THEATER

In the Restaurant: 3.6 – 5 KITCHEN SF / SEAT, 15 – 18 SF / PERSON

In the Theater: 7.5 SF / SEAT (FIXED SEATS), LOBBY 30% SEATING AREA

One space can dictate the planning requirements
of other required spaces.

SPACE PLANNING

IN MOST INSTANCES, THE BUILDING WILL
HOUSE A VARIETY OF SPACE TYPES

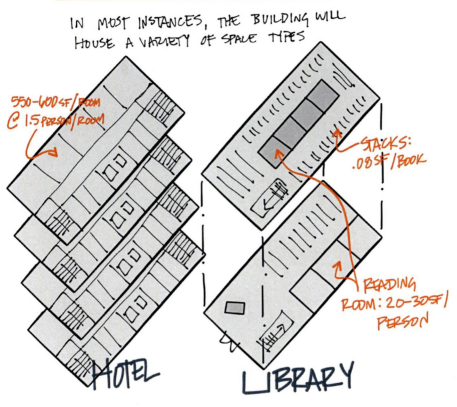

550-600 SF/ROOM
@ 1.5 PERSON/ROOM

STACKS:
.08 SF/BOOK

READING
ROOM: 20-30 SF/
PERSON

HOTEL   **LIBRARY**

There will typically be a variety of occupancy (use)
types in your building.

SPACE PLANNING

CODE DEFINES MINIMUMS ON SEATING TYPES

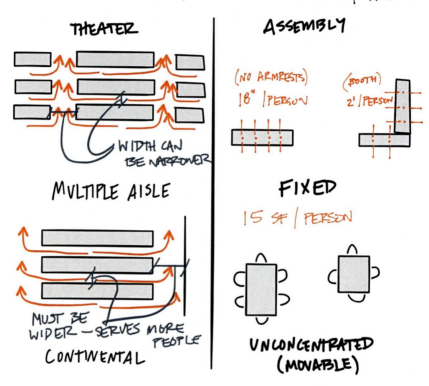

THEATER

WIDTH CAN BE NARROWER

MULTIPLE AISLE

MUST BE WIDER — SERVES MORE PEOPLE

CONTINENTAL

ASSEMBLY

(NO ARMRESTS) 18" / PERSON

(BOOTH) 2' / PERSON

FIXED

15 SF / PERSON

UNCONCENTRATED (MOVABLE)

Certain spaces have varying code minimums for seating.

FUNCTIONAL REQUIREMENTS

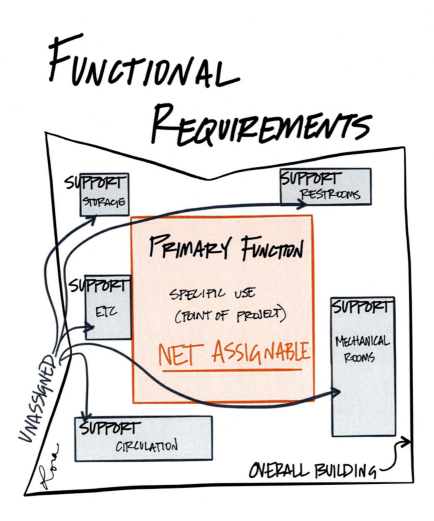

Assignable space = net = $$. Unassignable = support.

Functional Requirements

Gross Building Area

TOTAL
- UNASSIGNED
NET /TOTAL

NET TO GROSS RATIO

SUPPORT
STORAGE

SUPPORT
RESTROOMS

SUPPORT
ETC

PRIMARY FUNCTION

SPECIFIC USE
(POINT OF PROJECT)

SUPPORT

MECHANICAL ROOMS

SUPPORT
CIRCULATION

OVERALL BUILDING

The net-to-gross ratio helps determine efficiency and value.

Square Footage Efficiency
Depends on occupancy type & layout quality

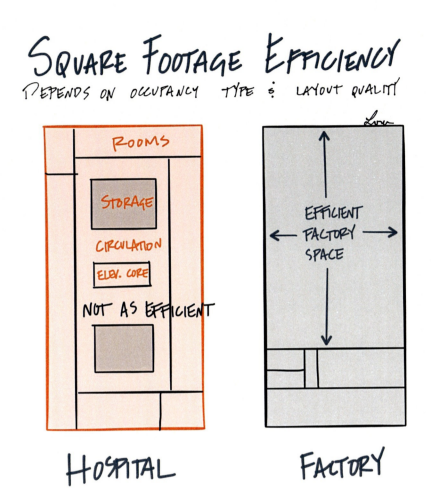

HOSPITAL

Rooms

Storage

Circulation

Elev. Core

Not as efficient

FACTORY

Efficient Factory Space

Square footage efficiency varies by use.

Square Footage Efficiency

STRONGLY CONSIDER LAYOUT

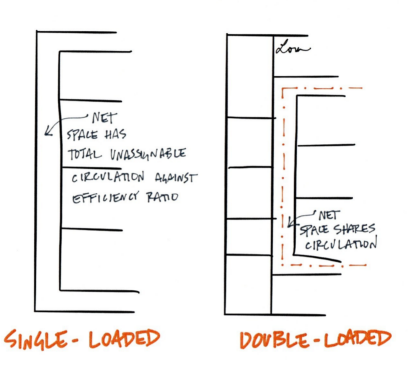

NET SPACE HAS TOTAL UNASSIGNABLE CIRCULATION AGAINST EFFICIENCY RATIO

Low

NET SPACE SHARES CIRCULATION

SINGLE - LOADED

DOUBLE - LOADED

Double-loaded corridors are more efficient.

SQUARE FOOTAGE EFFICIENCY
TYPICALLY 60 – 80% EFFICIENT

IF: NET USABLE SPACE IS ___50,000 SF___

AND: EFFICIENCY IS SET AT ___75%___

$\downarrow$

THEN: $GROSS = \dfrac{50,000}{.75}$

$GROSS = \pm 67,000 SF$

Square footage efficiency typically hovers between 60-80%.

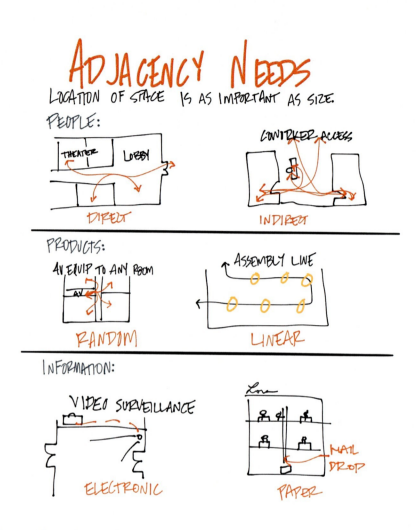

ADJACENCY NEEDS

LOCATION OF SPACE IS AS IMPORTANT AS SIZE.

PEOPLE:

THEATER | LOBBY

DIRECT

CONTRKER ACCESS

INDIRECT

PRODUCTS:

AV EQUIP TO ANY ROOM

AV

RANDOM

ASSEMBLY LINE

LINEAR

INFORMATION:

VIDEO SURVEILLANCE

ELECTRONIC

MAIL DROP

PAPER

Location is as important as size of space.

ADJACENCY MATRIX

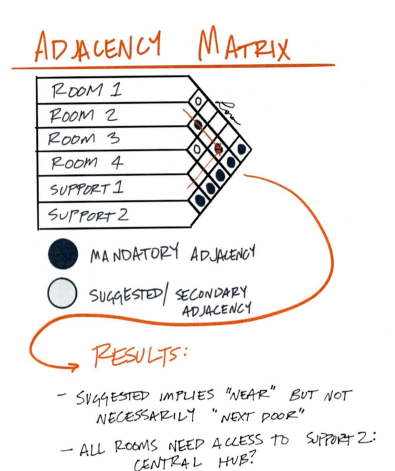

ROOM 1
ROOM 2
ROOM 3
ROOM 4
SUPPORT 1
SUPPORT 2

● MANDATORY ADJACENCY

○ SUGGESTED/ SECONDARY ADJACENCY

RESULTS:

- SUGGESTED IMPLIES "NEAR" BUT NOT NECESSARILY "NEXT DOOR"

- ALL ROOMS NEED ACCESS TO SUPPORT 2: CENTRAL HUB?

A matrix can help determine adjacencies.

ADJACENCY DIAGRAM

—VISUAL IMPLICATIONS OF MATRIX,
   OR STARTING POINT FOR DISCUSSION
* DOES NOT IMPLY ACTUAL SHAPE.

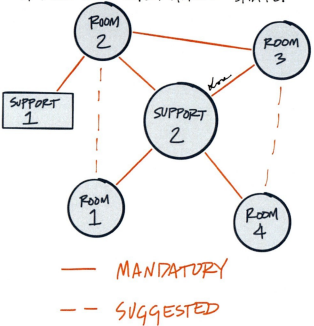

—— MANDATORY

– – SUGGESTED

Adjacency diagrams can create a starting point for design discussion.

PROGRAMMATIC CONCEPTS

Lisa

* NOT AN ACTUAL PHYSICAL SOLUTION

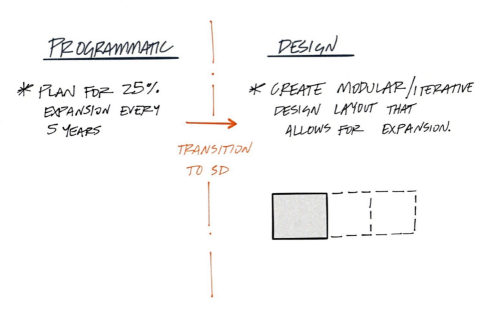

PROGRAMMATIC

* PLAN FOR 25%.
EXPANSION EVERY
5 YEARS

TRANSITION
TO SD

DESIGN

* CREATE MODULAR/ITERATIVE
DESIGN LAYOUT THAT
ALLOWS FOR EXPANSION.

Programmatic concepts answer questions that lead to design.

CONCEPTS

[LINEAR]

- IDENTICAL OR VARYING SIZE|SHAPE ANCHORED ALONG A SINGULAR LINE.
- CAN BE STRAIGHT, BENT, OR CURVED.
- EASILY MODULAR.

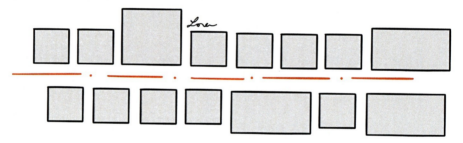

Linear organization occurs on a line: straight, bent, curved...but singular.

CONCEPTS

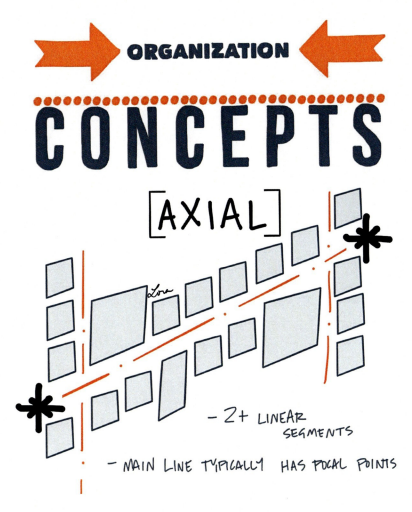

[AXIAL]

- 2+ LINEAR SEGMENTS
- MAIN LINE TYPICALLY HAS FOCAL POINTS

2+ lines intersecting creates axes, which then creates building shapes.

CONCEPTS

[GRID]

- STRONG PATTERN, BUT CAN BE MONOTONOUS
- SIZE CAN BE CHANGED FOR SPECIAL AREAS

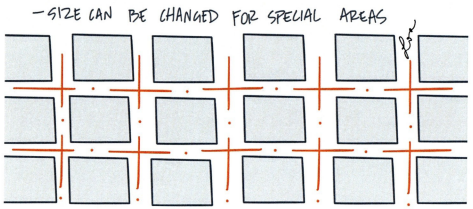

The grid is a strong pattern, but makes it hard to make a focal point within the building organization.

CONCEPTS

[CENTRAL]

- SINGULAR, RADIATING SPACE

- VERY FORMAL

- USED TOGETHER WITH LINEAR/AXIAL

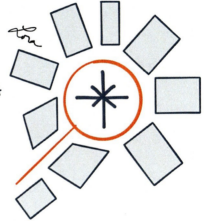

Unlike grids, central organizations work great for focal points.

ORGANIZATION

CONCEPTS

[RADIAL]

- 2+ RADIATING LINES
- CAN GROW INTO OTHER SHAPES

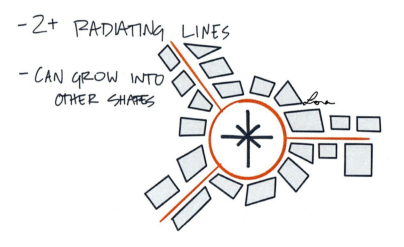

Radial patterns have a central hub with spokes like a wheel.

CONCEPTS

[CLUSTERED]

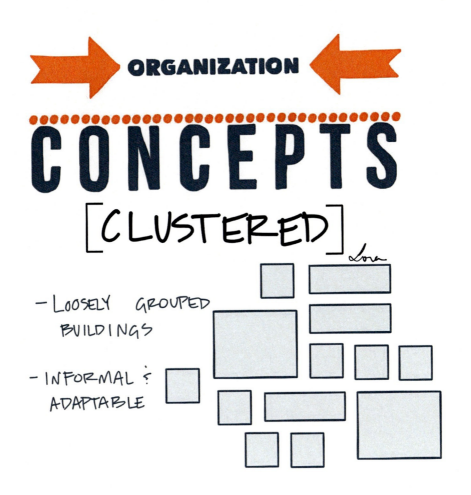

- LOOSELY GROUPED BUILDINGS

- INFORMAL & ADAPTABLE

Clustered layouts are informal and allow for growth over time.

CIRCULATION
{ PATTERNS }

- PRIMARY WAYS TO ORGANIZE A SPACE, BUILDING, OR GROUP OF BUILDINGS.

- MOVES PEOPLE, CARS, PRODUCTS, & SERVICES.

- HEIRARCHY OF PATHS.

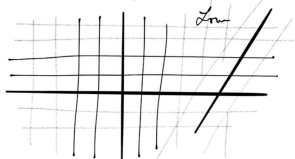

Patterns provide hierarchy for people, cars, and spaces.

CIRCULATION
{ PATTERNS }

—SOMETIMES SEPARATION OF CIRCULATION SPACES IS IMPORTANT.

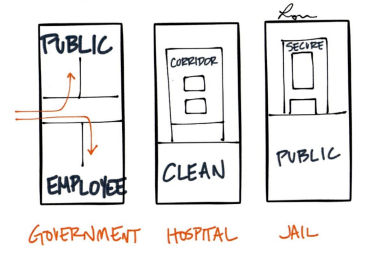

GOVERNMENT   HOSPITAL   JAIL

There are certain instances where circulation shouldn't overlap.

CIRCULATION
{ PATTERNS }

- SIMPLE & EFFICIENT

- COMPROMISE BETWEEN ADJACENCY
    NEEDS & EFFICIENT
    CIRCULATION.

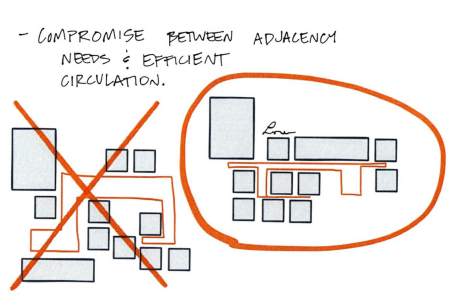

When it comes to building layout, there's always a compromise. That doesn't mean it should be a clusterf*.

CIRCULATION

{ & STRUCTURE }

[LINEAR → DUMBBELL]

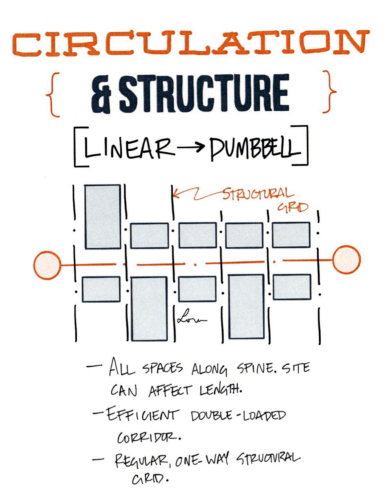

— ALL SPACES ALONG SPINE. SITE
   CAN AFFECT LENGTH.
— EFFICIENT DOUBLE-LOADED
   CORRIDOR.
— REGULAR, ONE-WAY STRUCTURAL
   GRID.

The dumbbell provides nodes at both ends with a linear center.

CIRCULATION
& STRUCTURE

[DOUGHNUT]

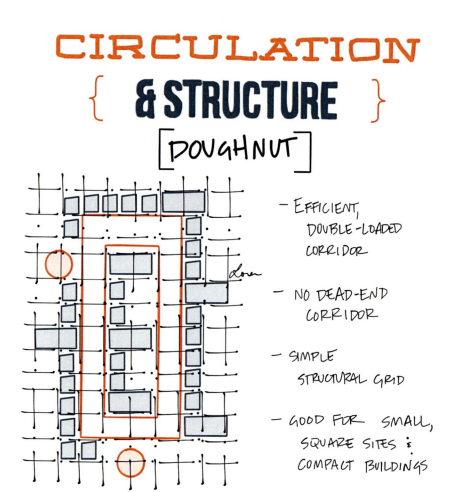

- EFFICIENT, DOUBLE-LOADED CORRIDOR

- NO DEAD-END CORRIDOR

- SIMPLE STRUCTURAL GRID

- GOOD FOR SMALL, SQUARE SITES & COMPACT BUILDINGS

Doughnut circulation is efficient and compact.

CIRCULATION

{ & STRUCTURE }

[DOUGHNUT & GRID]

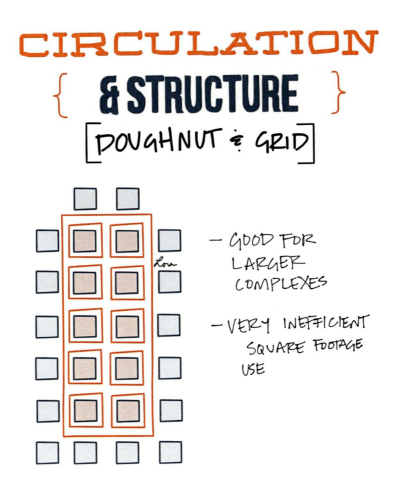

— GOOD FOR LARGER COMPLEXES

— VERY INEFFICIENT SQUARE FOOTAGE USE

A doughnut + grid layout is helpful when designing for larger complexes or campuses, but if it's a single building it is a very inefficient use of circulation space.

CIRCULATION

& STRUCTURE

[RADIAL]

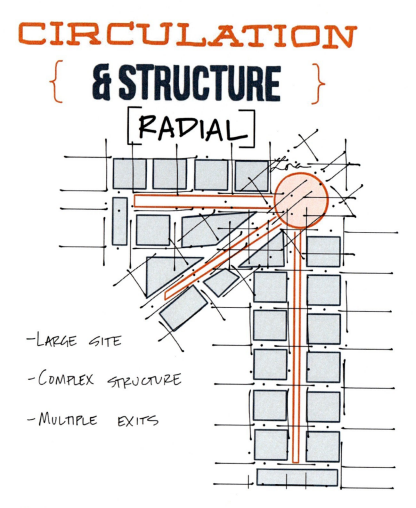

- LARGE SITE
- COMPLEX STRUCTURE
- MULTIPLE EXITS

Radial patterns create focal points but take up more space/structure.

CIRCULATION

{ **& STRUCTURE** }

[FIELD]

—INTENSIVE STRUCTURAL SYSTEMS

—NO STRONG DIRECTION. HARD TO ORIENT.

Field organization uses a lot of steel and has no hierarchy.

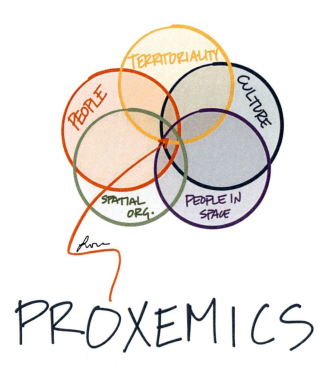

PROXEMICS

— CREATED BY EDWARD T. HALL

— INTERRELATION OF VARIOUS
THEORIES ON HUMAN
CULTURE & ACTIONS.

Proxemics is where it all comes together.

BEHAVIOR SETTING

- SPECIFIC PLACE
  - BOUNDARIES
  - OBJECTS
  - USE & TIME

} STANDARD

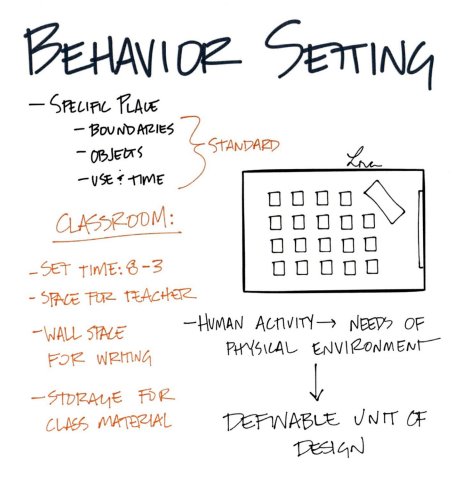

CLASSROOM:

- SET TIME: 8-3
- SPACE FOR TEACHER

- WALL SPACE
  FOR WRITING

- STORAGE FOR
  CLASS MATERIAL

— HUMAN ACTIVITY → NEEDS OF
    PHYSICAL ENVIRONMENT
        ↓
   DEFINABLE UNIT OF
      DESIGN

Behavior settings define the activities and needs
of an environment.

STATUS

─SYMBOLISM OF THE PHYSICAL ENVIRONMENT

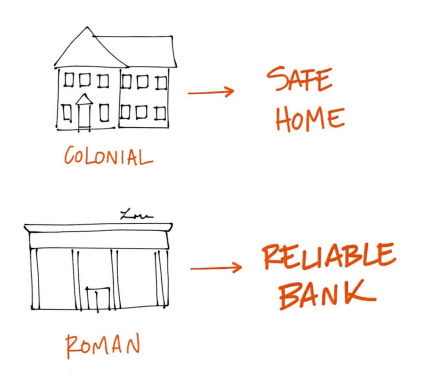

COLONIAL → SAFE HOME

ROMAN → RELIABLE BANK

Status symbols are formed early and often, even in architecture.

$ budgets $

PRO FORMA

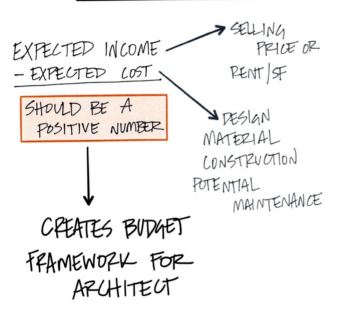

EXPECTED INCOME ———→ SELLING
− EXPECTED COST — PRICE OR
RENT/SF

SHOULD BE A POSITIVE NUMBER

→ DESIGN
MATERIAL
CONSTRUCTION
POTENTIAL
MAINTENANCE

CREATES BUDGET
FRAMEWORK FOR
ARCHITECT

A pro forma helps verify the financial health of a project and is sometimes required before a project can begin. (It's best practice to do whether required or not)

$ budgets $

Public Funding / Legislation

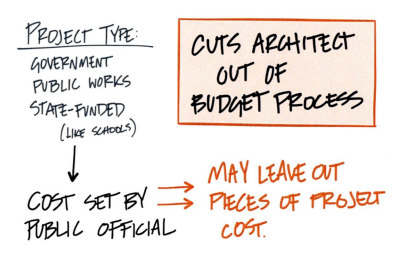

PROJECT TYPE:
GOVERNMENT
PUBLIC WORKS
STATE-FUNDED
(LIKE SCHOOLS)

↓

COST SET BY → MAY LEAVE OUT
PUBLIC OFFICIAL → PIECES OF PROJECT
COST.

CUTS ARCHITECT OUT OF BUDGET PROCESS

Public funding comes with restrictions and cuts the architect out of the budget process.

$ budgets $

ESTABLISHED BY ARCHITECT

BEST / MOST REALISTIC / ACCURATE
WAY TO BUDGET

↓

BASED ON SPECIFIC
PROJECT TYPE,
SITE, ETC

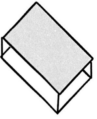

If a budget is established with the help of the architect, it has the best chances of being accurate.

cost influences
Lora

BUILDING COST

–ACTUAL COST OF
CONSTRUCTION

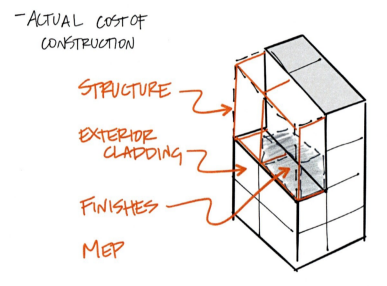

STRUCTURE

EXTERIOR
CLADDING

FINISHES

MEP

The actual cost of construction covers everything within the building.

cost influences
Lora

SITE DEVELOPMENT

- SEPARATE ITEM FROM
  BUILDING COST.
- IF VERY LARGE, MAY REQUIRE
  UPGRADES ADJACENT
  TO SITE.

FENCES

DRIVES

PARKING

EXTERIOR
LIGHTING

Site development can carry substantial costs
depending on mitigation, water, temporary
structures, and material quality.

cost influences
Zora

MOVABLE EQUIPMENT

- CAN POTENTIALLY BE A SEPARATE PROJECT/BUDGET
- ALSO KNOWN AS FFE
  (FURNITURE, FIXTURES,: EQUIPMENT)

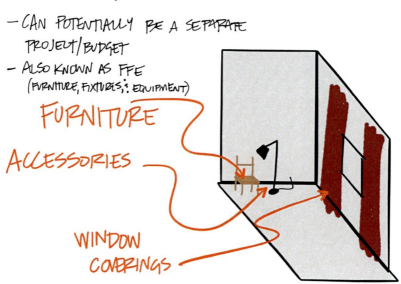

FURNITURE

ACCESSORIES

WINDOW
COVERINGS

Movable equipment can be part of a project's budget or it's own separate project.

cost influences
Lora

Professional Services

- ARCHITECTURE & ENGINEERING FEES
- TOPOGRAPHIC SURVEYS
- SOIL TESTS
- SPECIAL CONSULTANTS
- APPRAISALS & LEGAL FEES

> CAN BE UP TO 20%
> OF CONSTRUCTION COSTS

Professional services can account for up to 20% of a project's cost depending on depth and complexity of the project.

cost influences
Lora

INFLATION & CONTINGENCY

COST / TIME

PLAN FOR UNKNOWN COST OF MATERIALS OVER CALENDAR TIME OF CONSTRUCTION.

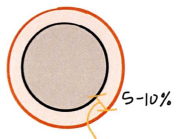

5-10%

CONTINGENCY PROVIDES FOR UNEXPECTED EXPENSES (LIKE UNDOCUMENTED ROCK OR HIGH DEMAND FOR GLASS)

Every project should plan for inflation of costs over the lifespan of construction. Contingency helps do this.

cost influences
Lora

PRELIMINARY BUDGETING

HOME → 150-200   TYPICALLY A GOOD GUESS BASED ON COST/SF

COLLEGE DORM → 250-300

CONCERT HALL → 375+

When determining a preliminary budget, a typical cost per square foot can be used based on project type.

BUDGETS
Love

PROJECT COMPARISON METHOD

WORKS WELL WITH LARGER COMPANIES WHO HAVE OTHER PROPERTIES FROM WHICH TO PULL DATA.

- 15-25% ACCURATE
- LOW, MID, & HIGH BUDGETS PROVIDED

COST PER BED

HOSPITAL

COST PER STUDENT

DORM

COST PER ROOM

HOTEL

The project comparison method helps set cost standards for project types based on past portfolio of work.

BUDGETS
Love

AREA / VOLUME METHOD

– SCHEMATIC DESIGN
   IS DONE

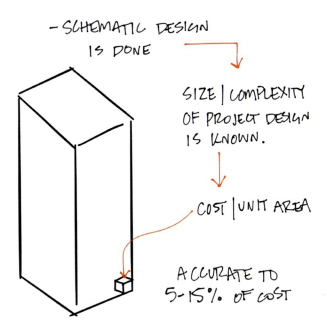

SIZE | COMPLEXITY
OF PROJECT DESIGN
IS KNOWN.

COST | UNIT AREA

ACCURATE TO
5-15% OF COST

The area/volume method is a more in-depth look at the cost per square foot after schematic design.

BUDGETS
Love

ASSEMBLY/SYSTEM METHOD

—SPACE/CONFIGURATION
OF BUILDING OR SITE IS KNOWN

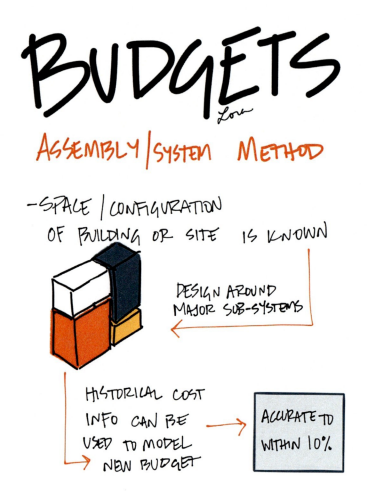

DESIGN AROUND
MAJOR SUB-SYSTEMS

HISTORICAL COST
INFO CAN BE
USED TO MODEL
NEW BUDGET

ACCURATE TO
WITHIN 10%.

The assembly/system method of budgeting can be done after a better idea of the spatial configuration and building systems are known.

BUDGETS
Lou

PARAMETER METHOD

- LATE SDs — EARLY CDs.

- EXPANDED ITEMIZATION.

~~FLOORING~~

CARPET
TILE
CONCRETE
TERRAZZO

Parameter method starts to list out all materials
and their typical costs per amount on the project.

BUDGETS
Love

MATRIX COSTING METHOD

– COST BREAKDOWN TO COMPONENT

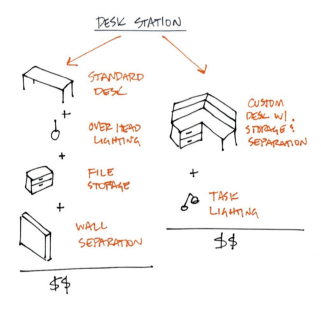

DESK STATION

STANDARD DESK

OVER HEAD LIGHTING

+

FILE STORAGE

+

WALL SEPARATION

$$

CUSTOM DESK W/ STORAGE & SEPARATION

+

TASK LIGHTING

$$

Matrix costing compares options based on what it would take to get to an equal finish.

OVERHEAD

10-20% OF TOTAL COST

GENERAL

COSTS OF RUNNING
A BUSINESS
- RENT/MORTGAGE
- STAFF
- UTILITIES
- ADVERTISING FEES
- RECURRING COSTS

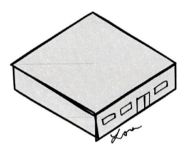

PROJECT

COSTS OF COMPLETING
A PROJECT
- TEMP OFFICES
- PHONES
- FACILITIES
- TRASH REMOVAL
- INSURANCE
- PERMITS
- TEMP UTILITIES

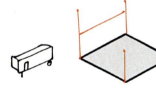

Overhead accounts for 10-20% of a project cost, both in the office and on site.

PROFIT for

DEPENDS ON PROJECT TYPE, SIZE,
RISK, MARKET CONDITIONS,
& DESIRED INCOME.

5-20%
OF JOB COST

COMBINED OVERHEAD & PROFIT
UP TO

15-40%

Profit on a project can be 5-20% of a project,
depending on size, type, recognition, and
complexity.

INFLATION

BASED ON A BASIS OF 1,000.
SIMILAR TO COST OF LIVING.

(NUMBERS ABOVE ARE MADE UP)

Inflation affects the cost of materials based on geography, similar to standard of living.

SCHEDULE

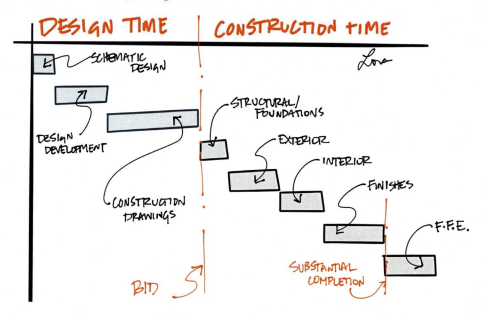

Typically a schedule is separated between design time and construction time.

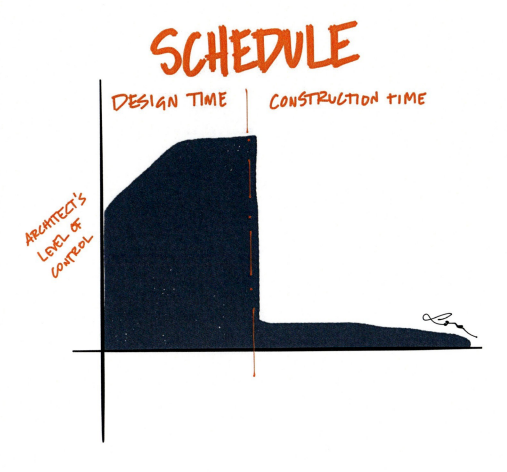

SCHEDULE

DESIGN TIME | CONSTRUCTION TIME

ARCHITECT'S LEVEL OF CONTROL

The architect's level of control decreases significantly when construction begins.

SCHEDULE

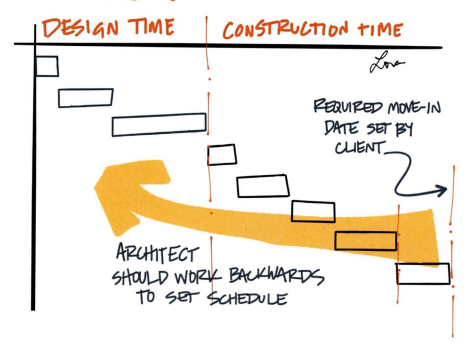

If there is a set move-in date required by the owner, the architect should work backwards to set the schedule.

SCHEDULE

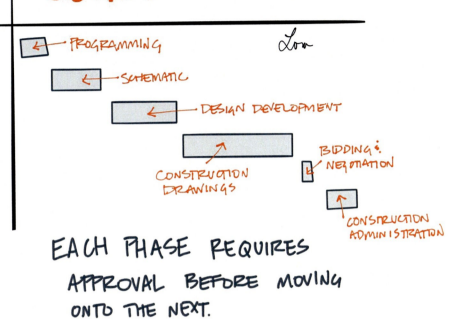

PROGRAMMING   *Low*

SCHEMATIC

DESIGN DEVELOPMENT

CONSTRUCTION DRAWINGS

BIDDING & NEGOTIATION

CONSTRUCTION ADMINISTRATION

EACH PHASE REQUIRES APPROVAL BEFORE MOVING ONTO THE NEXT.

On most projects, each phase of design requires approval (written) before moving onto the next phase.

SCHEDULE

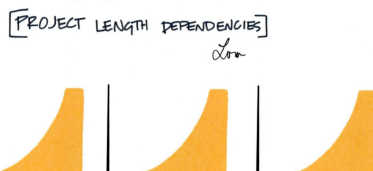

[PROJECT LENGTH DEPENDENCIES]

Low

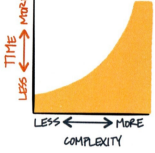

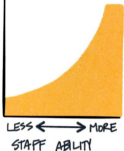

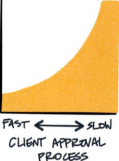

Project length can depend on a variety of things: complexity, number of people on the project, and how quickly and collaboratively the client responds.

SCHEDULE

[PROJECT LENGTH DEPENDENCIES]
Low

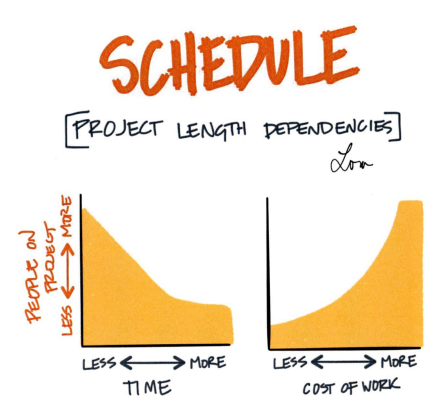

There are pros and cons to having more people on a project. It takes less time, but costs more in billable man hours.

SCHEDULE

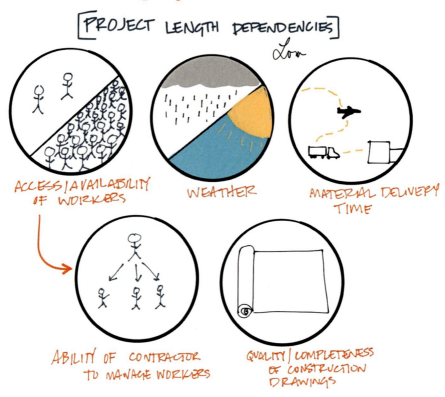

PROJECT LENGTH DEPENDENCIES

Low

ACCESS / AVAILABILITY OF WORKERS

WEATHER

MATERIAL DELIVERY TIME

ABILITY OF CONTRACTOR TO MANAGE WORKERS

QUALITY / COMPLETENESS OF CONSTRUCTION DRAWINGS

There are a variety of issues that affect the length of the project.

SCHEDULE

[CHART STYLES] Lou

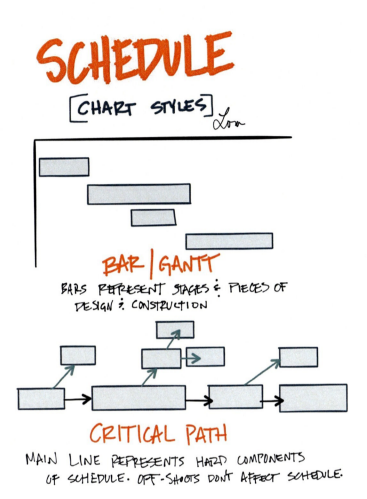

BAR / GANTT

BARS REPRESENT STAGES & PIECES OF
DESIGN & CONSTRUCTION

CRITICAL PATH

MAIN LINE REPRESENTS HARD COMPONENTS
OF SCHEDULE. OFF-SHOOTS DON'T AFFECT SCHEDULE.

There are different ways to represent the schedule: a bar/gantt chart and a critical path are the two main versions.

SCHEDULE

[FAST TRACK] Low

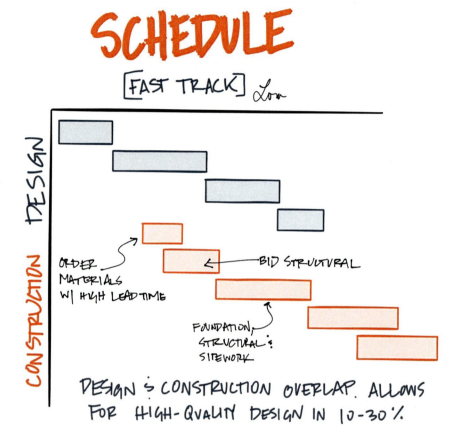

DESIGN

CONSTRUCTION

ORDER MATERIALS W/ HIGH LEAD TIME

BID STRUCTURAL

FOUNDATION, STRUCTURAL & SITEWORK

DESIGN & CONSTRUCTION OVERLAP. ALLOWS FOR HIGH-QUALITY DESIGN IN 10-30% OF TRADITIONAL TIME.

A fast track schedule overlaps design and construction with phasing.

CODES & REGULATIONS

A VARIETY OF REQUIREMENTS AFFECT
EACH PROJECT IN SMALL & LARGE WAYS.

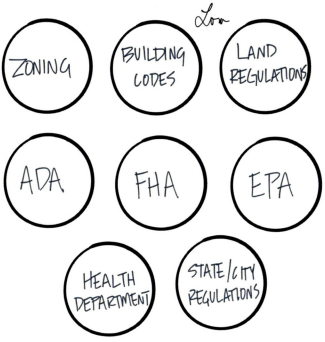

There are a variety of codes and regulations that impact a project. Be sure to verify that you are working within the constraints of each.